Math
Expressions

Volume 1

Developed by
The Children's Math Worlds Research Project

PROJECT DIRECTOR AND AUTHOR
Dr. Karen C. Fuson

This material is based upon work supported by the
National Science Foundation
under Grant Numbers
ESI-9816320, REC-9806020, and RED-935373.

Any opinions, findings, and conclusions, or recommendations expressed in this material
are those of the author and do not necessarily reflect the views of the National Science Foundation.

HOUGHTON MIFFLIN HARCOURT

Teacher Reviewers

Kindergarten

Patricia Stroh Sugiyama
Wilmette, Illinois

Barbara Wahle
Evanston, Illinois

Grade 1

Sandra Budson
Newton, Massachusetts

Janet Pecci
Chicago, Illinois

Megan Rees
Chicago, Illinois

Grade 2

Molly Dunn
Danvers, Massachusetts

Agnes Lesnick
Hillside, Illinois

Rita Soto
Chicago, Illinois

Grade 3

Jane Curran
Honesdale, Pennsylvania

Sandra Tucker
Chicago, Illinois

Grade 4

Sara Stoneberg Llibre
Chicago, Illinois

Sheri Roedel
Chicago, Illinois

Grade 5

Todd Atler
Chicago, Illinois

Leah Barry
Norfolk, Massachusetts

Special Thanks

Special thanks to the many teachers, students, parents, principals, writers, researchers, and work-study students who participated in the Children's Math Worlds Research Project over the years.

Credits

© Kerstin Layer/Age Fotostock

Illustrative art: Robin Boyer/Deborah Wolfe, LTD; Dave Clegg, Geoff Smith, Ron Mahoney, Tim Johnson
Technical art: Nesbitt Graphics, Inc.
Photos: Nesbitt Graphics, Inc.; Page 93 © C Squared Studios/Photodisc/Getty Images; Page 455 © Nick Green/Jupiter Images.

VOLUME 1 CONTENTS

Class Activity

▶ **Check Up for Additions**

Add.

1. 9 + 4 = ___	2. 6 + 3 = ___	3. 4 + 6 = ___	4. 7 + 7 = ___
5. 0 + 6 = ___	6. 7 + 1 = ___	7. 8 + 3 = ___	8. 8 + 9 = ___
9. 9 + 3 = ___	10. 6 + 4 = ___	11. 8 + 5 = ___	12. 5 + 4 = ___
13. 7 + 3 = ___	14. 5 + 6 = ___	15. 9 + 2 = ___	16. 5 + 5 = ___
17. 1 + 9 = ___	18. 8 + 2 = ___	19. 4 + 4 = ___	20. 3 + 6 = ___
21. 2 + 8 = ___	22. 9 + 1 = ___	23. 2 + 7 = ___	24. 3 + 8 = ___
25. 7 + 4 = ___	26. 4 + 5 = ___	27. 9 + 8 = ___	28. 6 + 8 = ___
29. 6 + 6 = ___	30. 9 + 5 = ___	31. 8 + 4 = ___	32. 1 + 6 = ___
33. 8 + 6 = ___	34. 6 + 7 = ___	35. 7 + 5 = ___	36. 8 + 8 = ___
37. 4 + 8 = ___	38. 7 + 9 = ___	39. 6 + 5 = ___	40. 9 + 6 = ___
41. 9 + 9 = ___	42. 3 + 7 = ___	43. 7 + 8 = ___	44. 4 + 7 = ___
45. 3 + 9 = ___	46. 7 + 6 = ___	47. 5 + 9 = ___	48. 7 + 8 = ___
49. 2 + 9 = ___	50. 5 + 7 = ___	51. 9 + 0 = ___	52. 5 + 8 = ___
53. 9 + 7 = ___	54. 6 + 0 = ___	55. 4 + 9 = ___	56. 6 + 9 = ___

Class Activity

► **Check Up for Subtractions**

Subtract.

1. 13 − 9 = __   2. 9 − 0 = __   3. 6 − 4 = __   4. 7 − 5 = __

5. 11 − 4 = __   6. 15 − 6 = __   7. 11 − 6 = __   8. 8 − 1 = __

9. 10 − 5 = __   10. 12 − 7 = __   11. 8 − 4 = __   12. 7 − 6 = __

13. 5 − 4 = __   14. 6 − 5 = __   15. 12 − 8 = __   16. 8 − 5 = __

17. 10 − 8 = __   18. 18 − 9 = __   19. 14 − 5 = __   20. 9 − 9 = __

21. 13 − 5 = __   22. 9 − 6 = __   23. 10 − 7 = __   24. 8 − 6 = __

25. 15 − 8 = __   26. 16 − 9 = __   27. 9 − 8 = __   28. 14 − 7 = __

29. 9 − 5 = __   30. 11 − 9 = __   31. 12 − 5 = __   32. 10 − 4 = __

33. 13 − 8 = __   34. 9 − 7 = __   35. 14 − 8 = __   36. 13 − 6 = __

37. 14 − 9 = __   38. 13 − 4 = __   39. 10 − 6 = __   40. 16 − 8 = __

41. 6 − 3 = __   42. 11 − 7 = __   43. 12 − 4 = __   44. 10 − 9 = __

45. 13 − 7 = __   46. 15 − 9 = __   47. 11 − 5 = __   48. 14 − 6 = __

49. 12 − 6 = __   50. 9 − 4 = __   51. 7 − 4 = __   52. 12 − 9 = __

53. 16 − 7 = __   54. 11 − 8 = __   55. 17 − 9 = __   56. 15 − 7 = __

Basic Additions and Subtractions

Vocabulary

place value

▶ Practice Place Value Drawings to 999

Write the number for each dot drawing.

1.
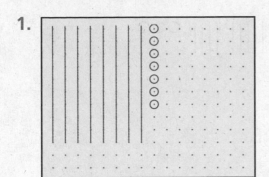

_____

2.
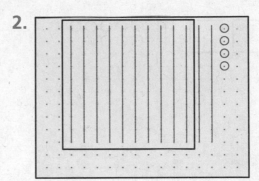

_____

Write the number for each place value drawing.

3. □ □ ||||| || ○○○○○ ○○

_____

4. □ □ □ ||||| | ○

_____

5. □ □ □ || ○○○
   □ □ □

_____

6. □ □ □ |||| ○○○○○ ○○○○
   □

_____

Make a place value drawing for each number.

7. 86

8. 587

Class Activity

Name _____ Date _____

▶ Practice with the Thousand Model

Write the number for each place value drawing.

9.

10.

_____   _____

Make a drawing for each number.

11. 2,368

12. 5,017

▶ Write Numbers for Word Names

Write the number for the words.

13. eighty-two _____

14. ninety-nine _____

15. four hundred sixty-seven _____

16. nine hundred six _____

17. one thousand, fifteen _____

18. eight thousand, one hundred twenty _____

Make Place Value Drawings

Dear Family,

Your child is learning math in an innovative program called *Math Expressions.* This program interweaves abstract mathematical concepts with everyday experiences of children. This approach helps children to understand math better.

In *Math Expressions* your child will learn math and have fun by:

- working with objects and making drawings of math situations

- working with other students and sharing problem-solving strategies with them

- writing and solving problems and connecting math to daily life

- helping classmates learn

Your child will have math homework almost every day. He or she needs a Homework Helper. The helper may be anyone — you, an older brother or sister (or other family member), a neighbor, or a friend.

Please decide who the main Homework Helper will be and ask your child to tell the teacher tomorrow.

Make a specific time for homework and provide your child with a quiet place to work. Encourage your child to talk about what he or she is doing in math class. If your child is having problems with math, please talk to me to see how you might help.

To make the concepts clearer, the *Math Expressions* program uses some special methods and activities. Two are described on the back of this letter.

Thank you. You are vital to your child's learning.

Sincerely,
Your child's teacher

continued ▶

- **Place Value Drawings:** Students learn to represent numbers with drawings that show how many hundreds, tens, and ones are in the numbers. Hundreds are represented by boxes. Tens are represented by vertical line segments. Ones are represented by small circles. The drawings are also used to help students understand regrouping in addition and subtraction. Here is a place value drawing for the number 178.

1 hundred   7 tens   8 ones

The 7 ten sticks and 8 circles are grouped in 5s so you can see the quantities easily and avoid errors.

- **Secret Code Cards:** Secret Code Cards are a set of cards for hundreds, tens, and ones. Students learn about place value by assembling the cards to show two- and three-digit numbers. Here is how the number 148 would be assembled.

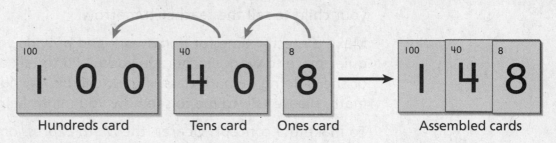

Hundreds card   Tens card   Ones card   Assembled cards

Make Place Value Drawings

Estimada familia:

Su niño está aprendiendo matemáticas por medio de un programa innovador llamado *Math Expressions.* Este programa relaciona conceptos matemáticos abstractos con la experiencia diaria de los niños. Esto ayuda a los niños a entender mejor las matemáticas.

Con *Math Expressions* su niño aprenderá matemáticas y se divertirá mientras:

- trabaja con objetos y hace dibujos de problemas matemáticos
- trabaja con otros estudiantes y comparte con ellos estrategias para resolver problemas
- escribe y resuelve problemas, y relaciona las matemáticas con su vida diaria
- ayuda a sus compañeros a aprender.

Su niño tendrá tarea de matemáticas casi todos los días. Le hará falta una persona que le ayude con la tarea. Esa persona puede ser usted, un hermano mayor (u otro familiar), un vecino o un amigo.

Por favor, decida quién será el ayudante principal y dígale a su niño que se lo informe al maestro mañana.

Establezca una hora para hacer la tarea y ofrezca a su niño un lugar tranquilo donde trabajar. Anime a su niño a comentar lo qué está aprendiendo en la clase de matemáticas. Si su niño tiene problemas con las matemáticas, por favor comuníquese conmigo para ver cómo puede ayudarlo.

Para presentar los conceptos de manera más clara, el programa *Math Expressions* usa métodos y actividades especiales. Dos de ellos se describen en el reverso de esta carta.

Gracias. Su ayuda es muy importante en el aprendizaje de su niño.

Atentamente,
El maestro de su niño

continúa ▶

- **Dibujos de valor posicional:** Los estudiantes aprenden a representar números por medio de dibujos que muestran cuántas centenas, decenas y unidades contienen. Las centenas están representadas con casillas, las decenas con segmentos de recta verticales y las unidades con círculos pequeños. Los dibujos también se usan para ayudar a los estudiantes a que comprendan cómo se reagrupa en la suma y en la resta. Éste es un dibujo de valor posicional para el número 178.

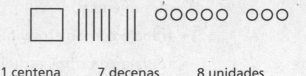

| 1 centena | 7 decenas | 8 unidades |

Los palitos de decenas y los círculos se agrupan en grupos de 5 para que puedan ver las cantidades más fácilmente y eviten errores.

- **Tarjetas de código secreto:** Las tarjetas de código secreto son un conjunto de tarjetas con centenas, decenas y unidades. Los estudiantes aprenden acerca del valor posicional organizando las tarjetas de manera que muestren números de dos y de tres dígitos. Así es como se puede armar el número 148.

| Tarjeta de centenas | Tarjeta de decenas | Tarjeta de unidades | Tarjetas organizadas |

Make Place Value Drawings

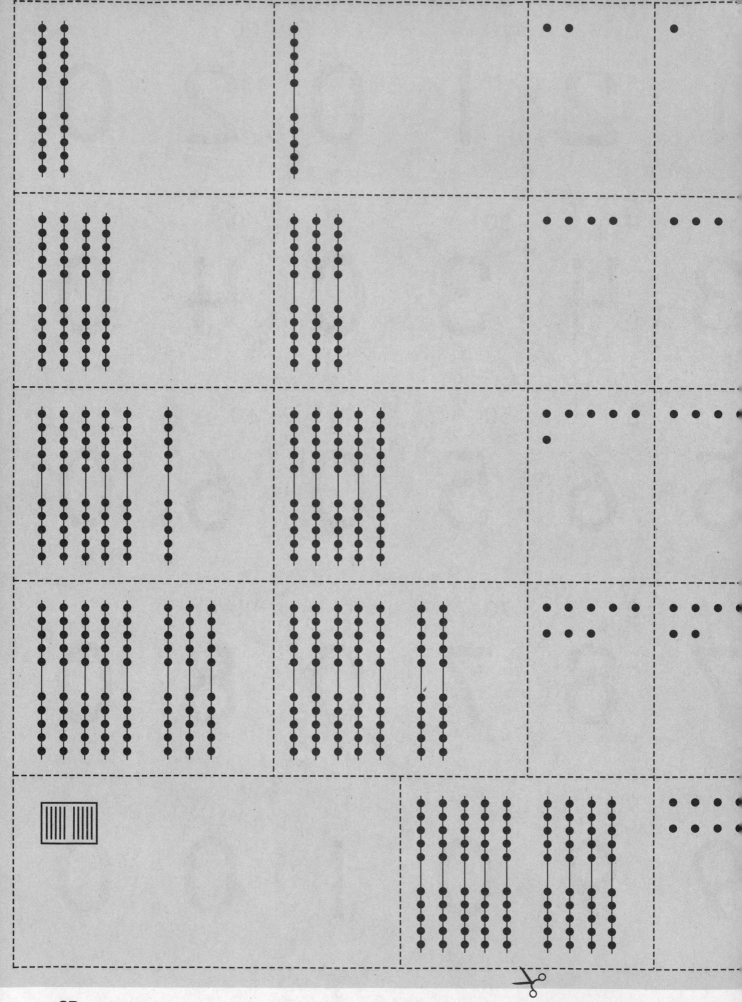

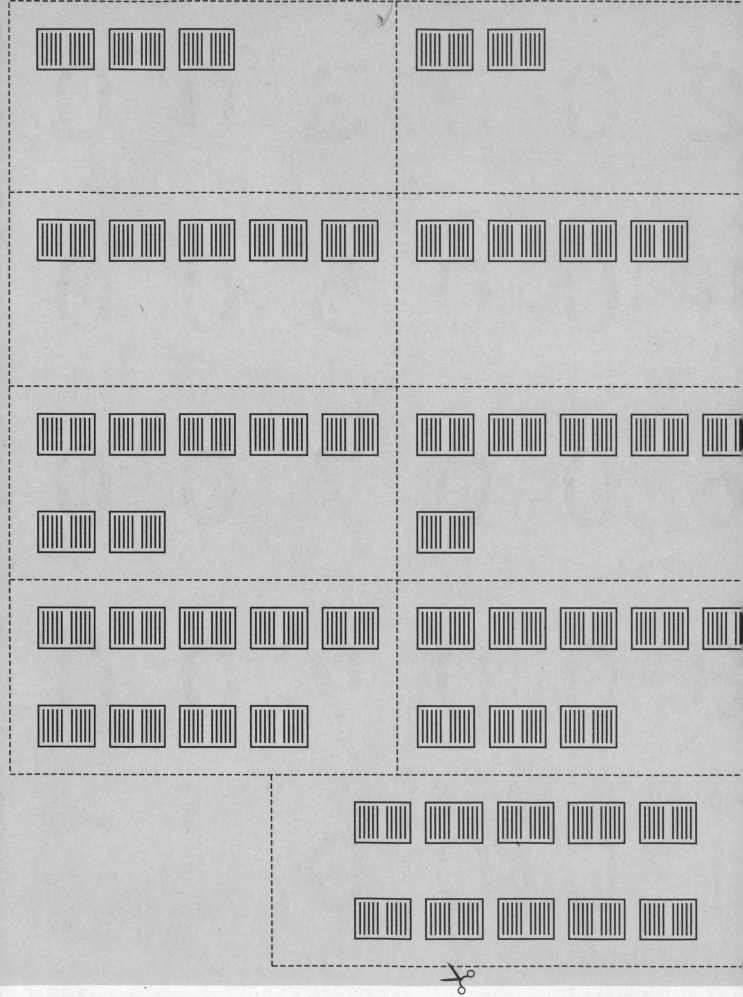

Class Activity

▶ Money Drawings on the Dot Array

On the dot side of your MathBoard, make a drawing to represent each money amount.

1. $1.84   **2.** $4.17   **3.** $3.03

▶ Money Drawings Without Dots

On the blank side of your MathBoard, make a drawing to represent each money amount.

4. $3.58   **5.** $6.29   **6.** $16.17

Write the money value for each drawing.

7.

_____

8.

_____

9.

_____

10.

_____

11.

_____

12.

_____

Name _____ **Date** _____

Going Further

▶ Numbers Through Ten Thousands

Write the place of the underlined digit. Then write its value.

1. 12,3<u>4</u>5 _____   2. 35,74<u>0</u> _____

3. 5<u>8</u>,436 _____   4. 89,7<u>8</u>2 _____

Write the word name for each number.

5. 43,875 _____

6. 75,086 _____

7. 98,502 _____

Write each number in expanded form.

8. 14,762 _____

9. 27,013 _____

10. 79,874 _____

Write the number in standard form.

11. 40,000 + 3,000 + 500 + 20 + 7 _____

12. 50,000 + 4,000 + 300 + 8 _____

13. 7 ten thousands + 6 hundreds + 5 ones _____

14. 9 ten thousands + 8 thousands + 4 hundreds + 7 tens _____

15. seventeen thousand, three-hundred ninety-five _____

16. eighty nine thousand, one hundred five _____

    Build Numbers and Represent Money Amounts

▶ Read and Write Numbers

Write the number for the words.

1. two hundred twelve _____   2. two thousand, eight _____

3. nine hundred ninety-one _____   4. six thousand, fifty-one _____

5. four hundred sixteen _____   6. six hundred nine _____

7. nine hundred eighty-seven   8. two thousand, eight

_____   _____

9. four thousand, seventeen   10. eight thousand, six hundred

_____   _____

Write the word name for each number.

11. 783   12. 907

_____   _____

13. 3,001   14. 8,043

_____   _____

Write each number in expanded form.

15. 314 _____   16. 2,148 _____

17. 7,089 _____   18. 8,305 _____

Write each number in standard form.

19. 5 thousands + 8 tens + 7 ones

_____

20. 6 thousands + 4 hundreds + 5 ones

_____

Class Activity

Name _____ Date _____

► Solve and Discuss

Show your work.

Use a place value drawing to help you solve each problem. Label your answers.

21. Scott baked a batch of rolls. He gave a bag of 10 rolls to each of 7 friends. He kept 1 roll for himself. How many rolls did he bake in all?

_____

22. Sixty-two bags of hotdog buns were delivered to the school cafeteria. Each bag had 10 buns. How many buns were delivered?

_____

Mario and Rosa baked 89 corn muffins.
They put the muffins in boxes of 10.

23. How many boxes did they fill?   24. How many muffins were left over?

_____   _____

Zoe's scout troop collected 743 cans of food to donate to a shelter. They put the cans in boxes of 10.

25. How many boxes did they fill?   26. How many cans were left over

_____   _____

27. **Math Journal** Write your own place value word problem. Make a drawing to show how to solve your problem.

Place Value in Word Problems

Class Activity

Vocabulary

place value

▶ **Scrambled Place Value Names**

Unscramble the place values and write the number.

1. 8 ones + 6 hundreds + 4 tens

_____

2. 9 hundreds + 7 tens + 1 one

_____

3. 5 ones + 0 tens + 7 hundreds

_____

4. 5 tens + 4 ones + 3 hundreds

_____

5. 2 tens + 2 hundreds + 2 ones

_____

6. 8 hundreds + 3 ones + 6 tens

_____

Unscramble the place values and write the number.
Then, make a place value drawing for the number.

7. 6 hundreds + 9 ones + 3 tens

_____

8. 9 ones + 3 tens + 8 hundreds

_____

9. 8 ones + 3 hundreds + 4 tens

_____

10. 2 hundreds + 9 tens + 1 one

_____

Class Activity

▶ Solve and Discuss

Solve each problem. Label your answer.

11. The bookstore received 35 boxes of books.
    Each box held 10 books. How many books did
    the store receive?

    _____

Maya's family picked 376 apples and put them
in baskets. Each basket holds 10 apples.

12. How many baskets did they fill?

    _____

13. How many apples were left over?

    _____

Aidee had 672 buttons. She put them in bags
with 100 buttons each.

14. How many bags did Aidee fill?

    _____

15. How many buttons were left over?

    _____

When Joseph broke open his piggy bank, there
were 543 pennies inside. He grouped the
pennies into piles of 100.

16. How many piles of 100 did
    Joseph make?

    _____

17. How many extra pennies did he
    have?

    _____

Dear Family,

Your child is currently participating in math activities that help him or her to understand addition and subtraction of 2- and 3-digit numbers.

Addition Methods: Students may use the common U.S. method, referred to as the New Groups Above Method, as well as two alternative methods. In the New Groups Below Method, students add from right to left and write the new ten and new hundred on the line. In the Show All Totals method, students add in either direction, write partial sums and then add the partial sums to get the total. Students also use proof drawings to demonstrate grouping 10 ones to make a new ten and grouping 10 tens to make a new hundred.

New Groups Below Method shows the number 13 better than does the New [Grou]ps Above Method, where the 1 and 3 [are s]eparated. Also, addition is easier in [New] Groups Below, where you add the [nu]mbers you see and just add 1.

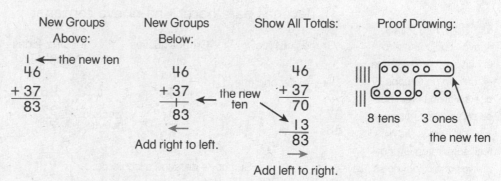

Subtraction Methods: Students may use the common U.S. method in which the subtraction is done right to left, with the ungrouping done before each column is subtracted. They also learn an alternative method in which all the ungrouping is done *before* the subtracting. If they do all the ungrouping first, students can subtract either from left to right or from right to left.

[U]ngroup First Method helps students [avoid] the common error of subtracting a [smalle]r top number from a larger bottom [numb]er.

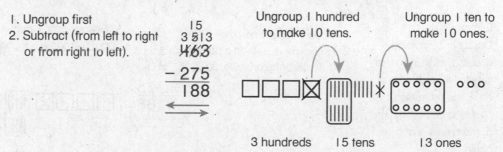

Please call if you have any questions or comments.

Thank you.

Sincerely,
Your child's teacher

Carta a la familia

Estimada familia:

En estos momentos, su niño está participando en actividades matemáticas que le ayudan a comprender la suma y la resta de números de 2 y de 3 dígitos.

Métodos de suma: Los estudiantes pueden usar el método común de los EE. UU., conocido como método de grupos nuevos arriba, y dos métodos alternativos. En el método de grupos nuevos abajo, los estudiantes suman de derecha a izquierda y escriben la nueva decena y la nueva centena en el renglón. En el método de mostrar todos los totales, los estudiantes suman en cualquier dirección, escriben sumas parciales y luego las suman para obtener el total. Los estudiantes también usan dibujos de prueba para demostrar cómo se agrupan 10 unidades para hacer una nueva decena, y 10 decenas para hacer una nueva centena.

El método de Grupos nuevos abajo muestra el número 13 mejor que el método de Grupos nuevos arriba en el que se separan los números 1 y 3. Además, es más fácil sumar con Grupos nuevos abajo, donde se suma los dos números que se ven y simplemente se añade 1.

Grupos nuevos arriba:

$$1 \leftarrow \text{la decena nueva}$$
$$\begin{array}{r} 46 \\ + 37 \\ \hline 83 \end{array}$$

Grupos nuevos abajo:

$$\begin{array}{r} 46 \\ + 37 \\ \hline 1 \\ 83 \end{array}$$ ← la decena nueva

Sumar de derecha a izquierda.

Mostrar todos los totales:

$$\begin{array}{r} 46 \\ + 37 \\ \hline 70 \\ 13 \\ \hline 83 \end{array}$$

Sumar de izquierda a derecha.

Dibujo de prueba:

la decena nueva

8 decenas 3 unidades

Métodos de resta: Los estudiantes pueden usar el método común de los EE. UU., en el cual la resta se hace de derecha a izquierda, desagrupando antes de restar cada columna. También aprenden un método alternativo en el que desagrupan todo *antes* de restar. Si los estudiantes desagrupan todo primero, pueden restar de izquierda a derecha o de derecha a izquierda.

El método de Desagrupar primero ayuda a los estudiantes a evitar el error común de restar un número pequeño de arriba a un número más grande de abajo.

1. Desagrupa primero.
2. Resta (de izquierda a derecha o de derecha a izquierda).

$$\begin{array}{r} 15 \\ 3\ 5\ 13 \\ \cancel{463} \\ - 275 \\ \hline 188 \end{array}$$

Desagrupar 1 centena para formar 10 decenas.

Desagrupar 1 decena para formar 10 unidades.

3 centenas   15 decenas   13 unidades

Si tiene alguna pregunta o comentario, por favor comuníquese conmigo. Gracias.

Atentamente,
El maestro de su niño

Explore Multi-Digit Addition

► Add Money

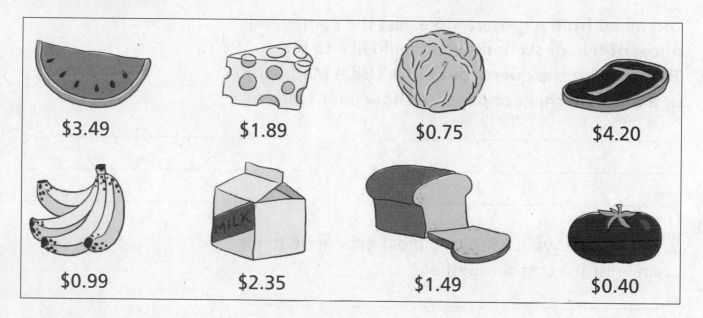

$3.49	$1.89	$0.75	$4.20
$0.99	$2.35	$1.49	$0.40

Use the pictures above to solve. Use a MathBoard or a separate sheet of paper to show your work.

1. Maria wants to buy milk and cheese. How much will the two items cost?

   _____

2. Arturo wants to buy a tomato and a steak. How much will Arturo's groceries cost?

   _____

3. Tamika wants to buy bananas and a watermelon. How much will she spend?

   _____

4. Choose two items. Which items did you choose? How much do they cost together?

   _____

   _____

   _____

Class Activity

▶ Add Money Amounts from a Grocery Store Ad

Use an ad from a grocery store. List the names and prices of five or six items you would like to buy. Then answer the questions below. Use a MathBoard or a separate sheet of paper to show your work.

_____   _____

_____   _____

_____   _____

5. How much would the two most expensive items on your list cost altogether?

   _____

6. How much would the two least expensive items cost in all?

   _____

7. What would be the total cost of your two favorite items?

   _____

8. Which items would you buy if you had $5.00 to spend?

   _____

9. Use the grocery ad to write and solve a word problem involving money.

   _____

   _____

   _____

   _____

Addition With Dollars and Cents

► Subtract and Check

Solve each problem.

1. Zane had $4.00. He bought a book for $3.76. How much money does he have left? Check by making a proof drawing. _____

2. Jasmine bought a cap. She paid with a $5.00 bill and got $1.62 in change. How much did the cap cost? Check by adding. _____

3. At the diner, Rita ordered the breakfast special for $2.91. She had $3.25 when she arrived at the diner. How much did she have after she paid her bill? Check by adding. _____

4. Bill bought a CD for $5.98. He paid with a $10.00 bill. What will his change be? Check by adding. _____

► Practice Deciding When to Ungroup

Answer each question.

| Adair subtracted 595 from 834. |

5. Did she have to **ungroup** to make more tens? Explain.

_____

_____

_____

6. Did she have to ungroup to make more ones? Explain.

_____

_____

_____

| Beatrice subtracted 441 from 950. |

7. Did she have to ungroup to make more tens? Explain.

_____

_____

_____

8. Did she have to ungroup to make more ones? Explain.

_____

_____

_____

| Wan subtracted 236 from 546. |

9. Did he have to ungroup to make more tens? Explain.

_____

_____

_____

10. Did he have to ungroup to make more ones? Explain.

_____

_____

_____

Going Further

Vocabulary
method
calculator
mental math

▶ Choose Mental Math, Pencil and Paper, or Calculator

Add or subtract. Then write what computation **method** you used. Write (p) for paper-and-pencil, (c) for calculator, or (m) for **mental math**.

1. $8.00
   − 7.50

   Method: _____

2. 79
   + 87

   Method: _____

3. 537
   − 91

   Method: _____

4. 495
   + 938

   Method: _____

5. $9.25
   − 4.01

   Method: _____

6. 2,000
   + 5,700

   Method: _____

7. $9,743
   − 5,221

   Method: _____

8. 12,534
   + 29,798

   Method: _____

9. $23,000
   − 14,000

   Method: _____

Solve each problem. Write whether you used paper-and-pencil, a calculator, or mental math.

10. Liz scores 20,000 points in her first turn. She scores 19,000 points on her second turn. How many points did she score altogether?

   _____

11. There were 17,948 people at the basketball game on Friday night. There were 16,777 people at the game on Saturday night. How many more people were there on Friday night than on Saturday night?

   _____

 12. **On the Back** Play the *Method Show-Down* game.

▶ Method Show-Down Game

Work in groups of three. Write the following methods on three separate index cards.

paper and pencil	mental math	calculator

To play the game.

1. Each student writes an addition or subtraction exercise using numbers up to 5 digits on an index card. Put the cards in a paper bag.

2. One student mixes the three method cards and distributes them to the group, while another student picks an exercise card from the paper bag. Each student then uses the method on his or her card to solve the problem. The first student to get the correct answer scores 1 point. Mental math may be really difficult for problems with large numbers.

3. Mix the method cards and repeat the activity. The first student to earn 5 points wins the game.

Practice Addition and Subtraction

Class Activity

Name _____ **Date** _____

► **Math and Literature**

Step 1: Make two spinners.

Spinner A   Spinner B

There are 46 stamps in a collection. There are 23 model cars in a collection. How many more stamps than model cars are there?

stamps   model cars

Step 2: Write names of collections on pieces of paper and put in a bag.

Step 3: Spin Spinner A twice to write a 2 or 3-digit number. Spin Spinner B twice to write a 2 or 3-digit number. Draw 1 or 2 collection names out of the bag.

Step 4: Use the numbers and collection names to write a word problem.

Act out the problems by modeling them on the MathBoard or with base ten blocks.

1. Write and solve a word problem using the rules above.

   _____

   _____

   _____

2. Sarah has 143 buttons. How many more buttons does she need to have 199 buttons?

   _____

3. Math Journal Write and solve more word problems about collections using the rules above.

   _____

▶ Rock, Paper, Scissors

Rock, Paper, Scissors is a game. The players show a rock, paper, or scissors with their hands.

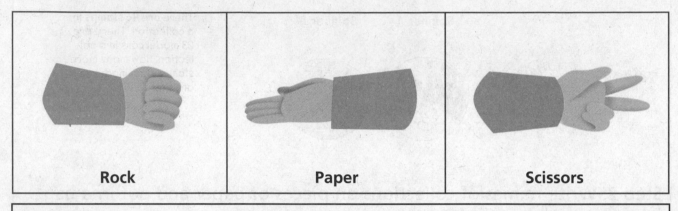

| Rock | Paper | Scissors |

Game Rules

1. The players throw their hand at the same time to show rock, paper, or scissors.

2. Rock crushes scissors and wins.

3. Scissors cuts paper and wins.

4. Paper covers rock and wins.

5. The player who scores a win gets 1 point.

6. If two players make the same throw with their hand, they must throw again.

7. The player with the most points wins.

4. List all of the different possibilities for one round if 2 players play the game?

_____

5. How many different possibilities are there?

_____

6. Play the game 10 times with a partner. Keep track of your results in a table. _____

Make a place value drawing for each number.

1. 57   2. 392

Unscramble the place values and write the number.

3. 9 ones + 6 hundreds + 4 tens   _____

4. 5 hundreds + 2 ones + 3 tens   _____

5. 5 ones + 7 hundreds + 1 thousand + 6 tens _____

6. 8 tens + 4 ones + 0 hundreds + 1 thousand _____

Write the number for the words.

7. eight hundred seventy-two _____

8. five hundred four   _____

9. one thousand fifty   _____

Add or subtract.

10. 435 + 283 = _____   11. 962 − 87 = _____

Name _____   Date _____

Add or subtract.

12.   972
       + 129
       _____

13.   617
       − 549
       _____

14.   800
       − 684
       _____

15. $3.29
       + 5.98
       _____

16. $5.31
       − 0.32
       _____

17. $10.00
       −   7.54
       _____

18. Gordon baked 346 blueberry muffins and 287 bran muffins. How many muffins did he bake in all?

_____

19. Write a subtraction word problem related to the addition word problem in problem 18. Then find the answer without doing any calculations.

_____

_____

_____

_____

20. Extended Response Veronica has 423 baseball cards. She put them in piles of 10 cards each.

How many piles of 10 cards did she make? _____

How many extra cards did she have?   _____

Explain your reasoning. _____

_____

_____

_____

Dear Family,

Your child will be learning about geometry during this school year. This first unit is about the geometric figures called quadrilaterals. These get their name because they have four (*quad-*) sides (*-lateral*).

Students will learn about four different kinds of quadrilaterals in this unit.

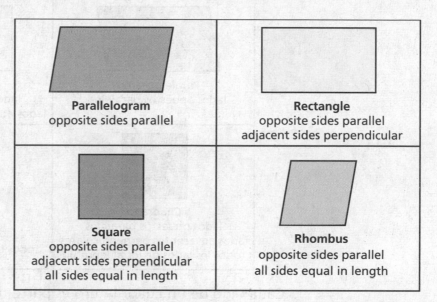

Parallelogram
opposite sides parallel

Rectangle
opposite sides parallel
adjacent sides perpendicular

Square
opposite sides parallel
adjacent sides perpendicular
all sides equal in length

Rhombus
opposite sides parallel
all sides equal in length

Each side of a quadrilateral is a part or a segment of a straight line. Your student will practice making careful measurements of line segments.

Students will measure line segments in centimeters in this unit. Centimeters are a convenient size for measuring and they are closely linked to the base 10 numeration system we use.

Your student will be able to recognize and describe different quadrilaterals by their sides. Some sides may be of equal length. Some sides may be parallel: they do not meet no matter how far they are extended. Some sides may be perpendicular: where they meet is like the corner of a square.

If you have any questions, please call or write to me.
Thank you.

Sincerely,
Your child's teacher

Carta a la familia

Estimada familia:

Durante este año escolar, su niño aprenderá geometría. La primera unidad se ocupa de figuras geométricas llamadas cuadriláteros. Éstas se llaman así porque tienen cuatro lados.

En esta unidad los estudiantes aprenderán acerca de cuatro tipos diferentes de cuadriláteros.

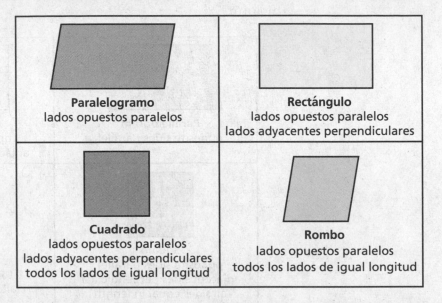

Paralelogramo
lados opuestos paralelos

Rectángulo
lados opuestos paralelos
lados adyacentes perpendiculares

Cuadrado
lados opuestos paralelos
lados adyacentes perpendiculares
todos los lados de igual longitud

Rombo
lados opuestos paralelos
todos los lados de igual longitud

Cada lado de un cuadrilátero es parte de un segmento de recta. Su niño practicará cómo medir segmentos de recta cuidadosamente.

En esta unidad los estudiantes medirán segmentos de recta en centímetros. Los centímetros son una medida apropiada y están directamente relacionados con el sistema numérico de base 10 que usamos.

Su niño podrá reconocer y describir diferentes cuadriláteros según sus lados. Algunos lados pueden tener la misma longitud. Algunos lados pueden ser paralelos: nunca se encuentran a pesar de lo largos que sean. Algunos lados pueden ser perpendiculares: cuando se encuentran, forman lo que podría ser el vértice de un cuadrado.

Si tiene alguna pregunta o comentario, por favor comuníquese conmigo. Gracias.

Atentamente,
El maestro de su niño

Measure Line Segments and Perimeters of Figures

Name _____

Date _____

▶ Identify Opposite and Adjacent Sides

Look at these quadrilaterals.

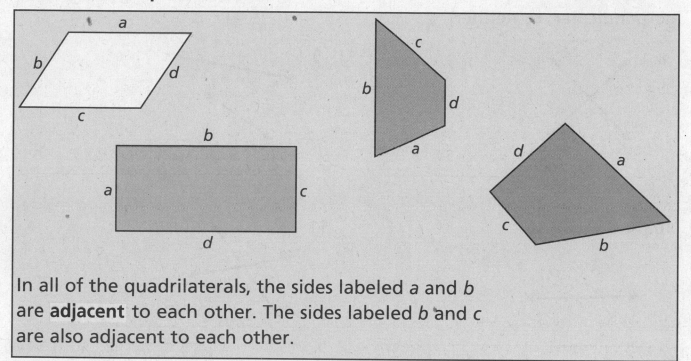

In all of the quadrilaterals, the sides labeled *a* and *b* are **adjacent** to each other. The sides labeled *b* and *c* are also adjacent to each other.

4. What do you think it means for two sides to be adjacent?

_____

_____

5. Which other sides are adjacent to each other?

_____

In all of the quadrilaterals, the sides labeled *a* and *c* are **opposite** each other.

6. What do you think it means for two sides to be opposite each other?

_____

_____

7. Which other sides are opposite each other?

_____

▶ Identify Types of Lines

Tell whether each pair of lines is parallel, perpendicular, or neither.

8.

_____

9.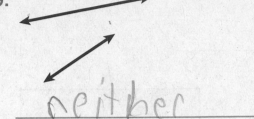

neither

10.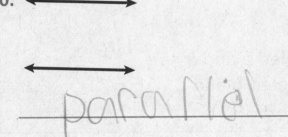

parallel

11.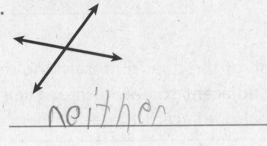

neither

12. Draw a pair of parallel line segments.

13. First, draw a line segment 3 cm long. Then, draw a line segment 6 cm long that looks perpendicular to your first line segment.

14. Name two perpendicular adjacent sides in this figure.

_____

15. Name two parallel opposite sides in the figure.

_____

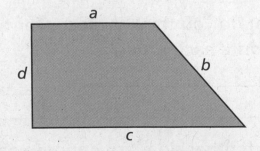

► Tangram Figures

Carefully cut out each figure along the dotted lines.
Make sure you cut as carefully and straight as you can.

Use your figures to create the patterns on Student
Activity Book page 63.

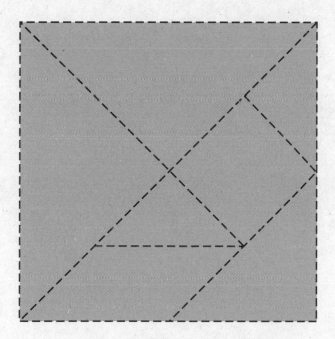

Tangram Figures

Going Further

Use your tangram figures from page 58A to make this cat. When you finish, draw lines to show how you placed the figures.

Try to create as many of these patterns as you can.

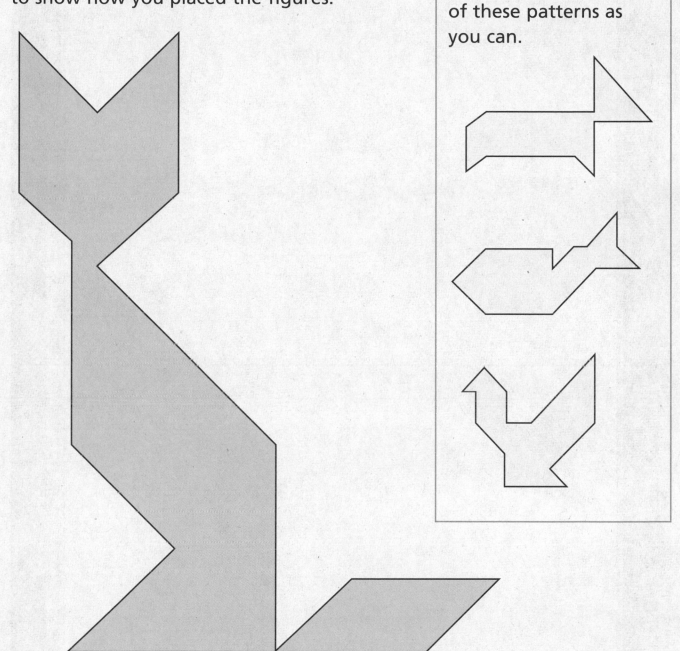

➡ **On the Back** Create your own pattern with tangrams and make a drawing of it.

Parallelograms, Rectangles, Squares, and Rhombuses

Find the perimeter of each figure. Use a centimeter ruler.

1.

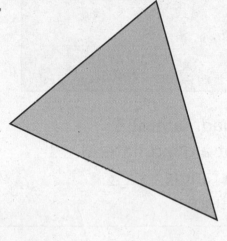

_____

2.

_____

Name each figure.

3.

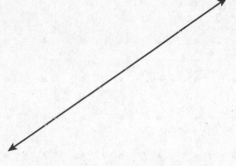

_____

4.

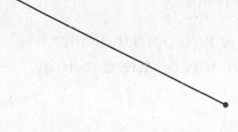

_____

Put a check mark beside every name that describes the figure.

5.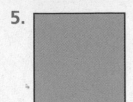

☐ quadrilateral
☐ not a quadrilateral
☐ rectangle
☐ square

6.

☐ quadrilateral
☐ not a quadrilateral
☐ rectangle
☐ square

7.

☐ quadrilateral
☐ not a quadrilateral
☐ rectangle
☐ square

8.

☐ quadrilateral
☐ not a quadrilateral
☐ rectangle
☐ square

9. Draw two perpendicular line segments on the dot array.

10. Extended Response Explain what it means for two line segments to be parallel. Draw an example.

_____

_____

► Represent Word Problems with Math Tools

The equations and Math Mountains below show the word problems on page 68.

Change Plus

$$8 + 6 = \boxed{}$$
Chris   Mom   total

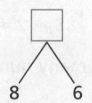

8   6

Change Minus

$$14 - 8 = \boxed{}$$
total   ate   now

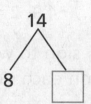

14

8    $\boxed{}$

Put Together

$$7 + 5 = \boxed{}$$
Alison   Taylor   total

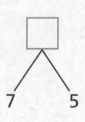

7   5

Take Apart

$$12 - 7 = \boxed{}$$
total   table   cooler

$$7 + \boxed{} = 12$$
table   cooler   total

12

7    $\boxed{}$

7. Write the unknown numbers in the boxes.

8. How are these math tools the same? How are they different?

_____

9. **Math Journal** Write a word problem for this equation: $11 - 4 = \boxed{}$. Then solve it.

Class Activity

Name _____ Date _____

Vocabulary

expression
equation

▶ Discuss the = and ≠ Signs

An **expression** is a combination of numbers, variables, and/or operation signs. Expressions do not have an equal sign.

An **equation** is made up of two equal quantities or expressions. An equal sign (=) is used to show that the two sides are equal.

$$8 = 5 + 3 \qquad 4 + 2 = 6 \qquad 7 = 7 \qquad 3 + 2 = 2 + 3 \qquad 6 - 2 = 1 + 1 + 2$$

The "is not equal to" sign (≠) shows that two quantities are not equal.

$$7 \neq 5 + 3 \qquad 4 + 2 \neq 8 \qquad 7 \neq 6 \qquad 6 - 2 \neq 2 + 3 \qquad 5 + 2 \neq 1 + 1 + 3$$

10. Use the = sign to write four equations. Vary how many numbers you have on each side.

$7 = 7$

$7 = 5 + 2$

$4 + 3 = 4 + 3$

$7 = 2 + 2 + 3$

11. Use the ≠ sign to write four "is not equal to" statements. Vary how many numbers you have on each side.

$6 \neq 5$ $7 \neq 1 + 1$

$2 + 3 \neq 4$

$3 \neq 5$

Write a number to make the number sentence true.

12. $16 = \boxed{7} + 9$

13. $3 + \boxed{5} \neq 12$

14. $7 + 2 = 2 + \boxed{7}$

15. $15 - \boxed{8} = 7$

16. $\boxed{5} \neq 14 - 7$

17. $6 - 2 \neq 1 + 1 + \boxed{10}$

Write = or ≠ to make a true number sentence.

18. $8 + 2 + 4 \underline{=} 9 + 5$

19. $8 \underline{\neq} 6 - 2$

20. $7 \underline{\supset} 4 + 3$

Addition and Subtraction Situations

Dear Family,

In this unit, your child will solve addition and subtraction word problems involving a total and two partners.

- If one of the partners is unknown, it can be found by subtracting the known partner from the total or by counting on from the known partner to the total.

- If the total is unknown, it can be found by adding the partners.

Math Mountains are used to show a total and two partners. Students can use the Math Mountain to write an equation and then solve the equation to find the unknown.

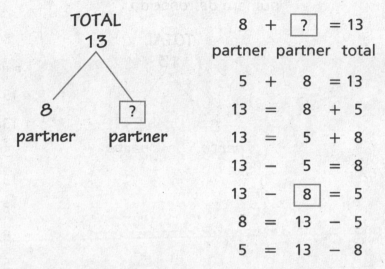

$$8 \ + \ \boxed{?} \ = 13$$

partner partner total

$$5 + 8 = 13$$
$$13 = 8 + 5$$
$$13 = 5 + 8$$
$$13 - 5 = 8$$
$$13 - \boxed{8} = 5$$
$$8 = 13 - 5$$
$$5 = 13 - 8$$

Equations with numbers alone on the left are also emphasized to help with the understanding of algebra.

Comparison Bars are used to solve problems that involve one amount that is more than or less than another amount. Making Comparison Bars can help a student organize the information in the problem in order to find the unknown smaller amount, larger amount, or the difference.

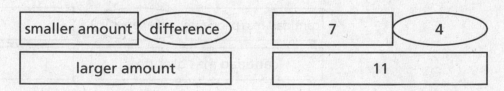

Please call or write if you have any questions or comments.

Sincerely,
Your child's teacher

Carta a la familia

Estimada familia:

En esta unidad, su niño resolverá problemas verbales de suma y resta que contienen un total y dos partes.

• Si no se conoce una de las partes, se la puede hallar restando la parte conocida del total o contando hacia adelante desde la parte conocida hasta el total.

• Si no se sabe el total, se lo puede hallar sumando las partes.

Para mostrar un total y dos partes se usan **montañas matemáticas**. Los estudiantes pueden usar *montañas matemáticas* para escribir una ecuación y luego resolverla para hallar el número desconocido.

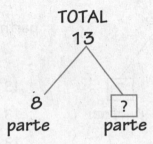

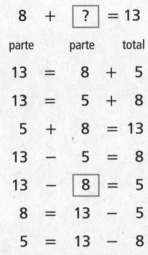

$$8 + \boxed{?} = 13$$

parte	parte	total

$$13 = 8 + 5$$
$$13 = 5 + 8$$
$$5 + 8 = 13$$
$$13 - 5 = 8$$
$$13 - \boxed{8} = 5$$
$$8 = 13 - 5$$
$$5 = 13 - 8$$

Se les da énfasis a las ecuaciones que tienen los números solos en el lado izquierdo, para facilitar la comprensión del álgebra.

Para resolver problemas que contengan una cantidad mayor o menor que otra se pueden usar **barras de comparación**. Estas *barras de comparación* pueden ayudar al estudiante a organizar la información que se presenta en el problema para hallar la cantidad más pequeña desconocida, la más grande o la diferencia.

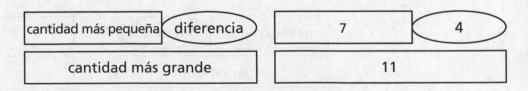

Si tiene alguna pregunta o comentario, por favor comuníquese conmigo.

Atentamente,
El maestro de su niño

Addition and Subtraction Situations

▶Discuss Comparison Problems

Solve each problem. Label your answers.

> David has 5 marbles. Ana has 8 marbles.

1. How many more marbles
   does Ana have than David? _____

2. How many fewer marbles
   does David have than Ana? _____

Here are two ways to represent the comparison situation.

Comparison Drawing

David ○○○○○

Ana ○○○○○○○○

Comparison Bars

| David | 5 | ? |
| Ana | 8 | |

> Claire has 8 marbles. Sasha has 15 marbles.

3. How many more marbles does
   Sasha have than Claire? _____

4. How many fewer marbles does
   Claire have than Sasha? _____

Show your work.

> Rocky has 7 fishing lures. Megan has 12 fishing lures.

5. How many fewer fishing
   lures does Rocky have
   than Megan? _____

Class Activity

▶ **Find an Unknown Larger or Smaller Amount**

Solve each problem. Label your answers.   *Show your work.*

6. **Unknown Larger Amount** Maribel has 8 stickers.
   Arnon has 3 more stickers than Maribel. How
   many stickers does Arnon have?

   _____

7. **Unknown Smaller Amount** Arnon has 11 stickers.
   Maribel has 3 fewer stickers than Arnon. How
   many stickers does Maribel have?

   _____

8. **Unknown Larger Amount** Ivan has 9 goldfish.
   Milo has 5 more goldfish than Ivan. How many
   goldfish does Milo have?

   _____

9. **Unknown Smaller Amount** Milo has 14 goldfish.
   Ivan has 5 fewer goldfish than Milo. How many
   goldfish does Ivan have?

   _____

Class Activity

Name _____   Date _____

▶ The Puzzled Penguin

Dear Math Students,

As part of my math homework, I solved this problem:

Carlos has 9 fish. He has 4 fewer fish than Daniel. How many fish does Daniel have?

Here is what I did: $9 - 4 = 5$ Daniel has 5 fish.

Is my answer right? If not, please correct my work, and tell what I did wrong.

Sincerely,
The Puzzled Penguin

▶ Solve Comparison Problems with Misleading Language

Solve each problem on a separate piece of paper.

1. Unknown Smaller Amount Daniel has 13 fish. Daniel has 4 more fish than Carlos. How many fish does Carlos have?

_____

2. Unknown Larger Amount Gina ran 8 laps. She ran 6 fewer laps than Bettina. How many laps did Bettina run?

_____

3. Unknown Smaller Amount Bettina ran 14 laps. Bettina ran 6 more laps than Gina. How many laps did Gina run?

_____

4. Sara read 8 books this month. She read 6 fewer books than Lupe. How many books did Lupe read this month?

_____

▶ Solve Comparison Problems Without the Words *More* or *Fewer*

Solve each problem. Label your answers.

Show your work.

5. The coach brought 8 hockey sticks to practice. There were 13 players at practice. How many players didn't get sticks?

   _____

6. At a meeting, 5 people had to stand because there were not enough chairs. There were 12 chairs. How many people came to the meeting?

   _____

7. Jess had 16 apples. After he gave one to each of his cousins, he had 3 apples left. How many cousins does Jess have?

   _____

8. At the park, 4 of the children could not swing because there were not enough swings. There were 10 children at the park. How many swings were on the swing set?

   _____

9. Maile took one step on each tile along the garden path. After she took 14 steps, there were 3 more tiles left to go. How many tiles were there along the path?

   _____

▶Solve Multi-Digit Problems with Unknown Partners

Solve each problem. Label your answers. Use your MathBoard or another sheet of paper.

1. Amanda had 783 seashells in her collection. She found some more seashells at the beach. Now she has 912 seashells. How many seashells did she find at the beach?

   _____

2. Michelle and Sanjay are playing pinball. Together they have scored 1,509 points. Michelle has scored 718 points. How many points has Sanjay scored?

   _____

3. Beth and Olivia are driving across the country. Beth drove 923 miles. Together they drove 1,586 miles. How many miles did Olivia drive?

   _____

4. There were 1,936 people at a baseball game. A number of people left during the sixth inning. There were 856 people at the game after the sixth inning. How many people left during the sixth inning?

   _____

Class Activity

▶Solve Multi-Digit Problems with Unknown Starts

Solve each problem. Label your answers.

Show your work.

5. The students at Oakdale School collected some cans of food in May. They collected 978 cans of food in June. They collected 1,729 cans of food in all in those two months. How many cans of food did they collect in May?

_____

6. Mrs. Perez ordered some sheets of colored paper for her art class. Her students used 831 sheets of colored paper. There are 369 sheets left over. How many sheets of colored paper did Mrs. Perez order?

_____

7. Today a grocer sold 682 melons. At the end of the day, 756 melons were left over. How many melons did the grocer have at the beginning of the day?

_____

8. Mr. Chung's class earned some money selling pizzas last month. This month, Mr. Chung's class earned $562 more. Now they have $986. How much money did the class earn last month?

_____

Multi-Digit Unknown Partner and Unknown Start Problems

Class Activity

▶Solve Mixed Problems

Solve each problem. Label your answers.

Show your work.

9. A book has 876 pages. Maria has read 456 pages of the book. How many more pages must Maria read to finish the book?

_____

10. Natalie polished some rocks in March. She polished 418 more rocks in April. She now has 682 polished rocks. How many rocks did Natalie polish in March?

_____

11. Today the visitors at the library checked out a total of 1,326 books. Of these books, 679 did not come from the children's section. How many books did come from the children's section?

_____

12. Jeffrey has a nickel collection. He put 368 nickels in the bank. He now has 283 nickels. How many nickels did Jeffrey start with?

_____

13. **Math Journal** Write a problem that can be solved using this equation: $\square + 156 = 215$. Then solve it.

Class Activity

Name _____   **Date** _____

Vocabulary
inequality

► Discuss Equations and Inequalities

An equation shows that two quantities or expressions are equal.
An equal sign (=) is used to show that the two sides are equal.

$$8 = 5 + 3 \qquad 4 + 2 = 6 \qquad 7 = 7 \qquad 3 + 2 = 2 + 3 \qquad 6 - 2 = 1 + 1 + 2$$

An **inequality** shows that two quantities or expressions are not equal. The signs less than (<), greater than (>), and not equal (≠) show that the two sides are not equal.

$$7 < 5 + 3 \qquad 9 + 2 > 8 \qquad 7 \ne 6 \qquad 6 - 2 < 2 + 3 \qquad 5 + 2 > 1 + 1 + 3$$

1. Use the > sign to write four inequalities. Vary how many numbers you have on each side.

   _____   _____

   _____   _____

2. Use the < sign to write four inequalities. Vary how many numbers you have on each side.

   _____   _____

   _____   _____

Write a number to make the inequality true.

3. $16 > \boxed{} + 9$ 4. $3 + \boxed{} > 12$ 5. $7 + 2 > 2 + \boxed{}$

6. $18 - \boxed{} > 9$ 7. $\boxed{} < 15 - 7$ 8. $5 - 2 < 1 + 1 + \boxed{}$

Write >, <, or = to make a true number sentence.

9. $5 + 2 + 4 \underline{} 9 + 5$ 10. $9 \underline{} 8 - 2$ 11. $12 \underline{} 7 + 5$

Multi-Digit Unknown Partner and Unknown Start Problems

Name _____

Date _____

► **Solve Multi-Digit Comparison Problems**

Solve each problem. Label your answers.

Show your work.

1. The Sunnytown Library has 1,052 history books. The Judson Library has 863 history books. How many more history books does the Sunnytown Library have than the Judson Library?

   _____

2. Today the Daisy Café used 465 plates. They used 197 fewer plates yesterday than they used today. How many plates did the Daisy Café use yesterday?

   _____

3. José received 749 votes in the school election. Cora received 126 more votes than José. How many votes did Cora receive?

   _____

4. Marco earned $428 doing yard work. Troy earned $186. How much less money did Troy earn than Marco?

   _____

▶ Solve Multi-Digit Comparison Problems with Misleading Language

Solve each problem. Draw comparison bars to help you. Label your answers.

5. Billy has 679 pennies. He has 278 more pennies than Lee. How many pennies does Lee have?

_____

6. Rebecca drove 362 miles. She drove 439 fewer miles than Fiona. How many miles did Fiona drive? _____

7. The baseball team gave 250 caps to people who came to the game today. There were 569 people at the game. How many people did not get a cap? _____

8. The principal bought 975 pencils at the beginning of the school year. Each student in the school received one pencil. The principal had 123 pencils left over. How many students are in the school? _____

Name _____ **Date** _____

▶Use Logical Reasoning to Solve Problems

Solve.

Show your work.

1. Darnell, Rita, and Mark each bought a CD. Mark spent $3 less than Darnell. Rita spent $7 more than Mark. Darnell spent $11. How much did Rita spend?

   _____

2. Helmer, Lily, and Pete live on Maple Street. Pete's house number is twice Helmer's. Lily's house number is 251. Helmer's house number is 45 less than Lily's. What is Pete's house number?

   _____

3. Luisa, Sally, and Tran each have a coin collection. Sally has 72 more coins than Luisa. Luisa has 126 fewer coins than Tran. Sally has 429 coins. How many coins does each have?

   _____

4. Tonya, Seth, Ann, and Len were in a walk-a-thon. They walked 14 mi, 26 mi, 19 mi, and 10 mi. Seth walked the farthest. Tonya walked farther than Len. Ann walked 10 mi. How far did each walk?

   _____

5. Dave, Shawna, Liz, and Matt are friends. Liz is taller than Shawna. Dave is the tallest. Matt is taller than Liz. What is their order from shortest to tallest?

   _____

6. **Math Journal** Explain the strategy you used to solve problem 5.

Going Further

▶ Choose the Equation

Circle the equation that represents the problem. Then solve.

7. Trinh had 9 pennies. Then he found some more pennies. Trinh has 17 pennies in all. How many pennies did Trinh find?

$17 - \boxed{} = 9$ $\qquad$ $9 + 8 = \boxed{}$ $\qquad$ $9 + \boxed{} = 17$

_____

8. There are 13 boys and girls at the park. 6 of the children are girls. How many boys are at the park?

$6 - 13 = \boxed{}$ $\qquad$ $6 + \boxed{} = 13$ $\qquad$ $13 + 6 = \boxed{}$

_____

9. Taci found some shells. Then she found 8 more shells. Taci has 14 shells. How many shells did Taci find at the beginning?

$\boxed{} + 8 = 14$ $\qquad$ $8 + 6 = \boxed{}$ $\qquad$ $14 - \boxed{} = 8$

_____

10. Miguel made some paper airplanes. He gave 5 of the paper airplanes to a friend. Miguel has 7 left. How many paper airplanes did he make?

$7 - 5 = \boxed{}$ $\qquad$ $\boxed{} - 5 = 7$ $\qquad$ $5 + 7 = \boxed{}$

_____

Multi-Digit Comparison Problems

Name _____ **Date** _____

▶Solve Mixed Multi-Digit Word Problems

Solve each problem. Label your answers.

Show your work.

1. Jacob had 219 bottle caps in his collection. Then he found some more. Now he has 347 bottle caps. How many bottle caps did Jacob find?

_____

2. Yesterday Tamara stamped some invitations. Today she stamped 239 invitations. She stamped 427 invitations in all. How many invitations did she stamp yesterday? _____

3. Batai made 122 calls in the phone-a-thon. Gina made 261 calls. How many more calls did Gina make than Batai? _____

4. Greta has 449 feet of fencing for her dog run. Mitch has 110 fewer feet of fencing for his dog run. How many feet of fencing does Mitch have? _____

Class Activity

Solve each problem. Label your answers.   *Show your work.*

5. The Grove Street bus carried 798 passengers today. The Elm Street bus carried 298 more passengers today than the Grove Street bus. How many passengers did the Elm Street bus carry today?

_____

6. Park City Cycle has 876 bicycles in stock. This is 134 more bicycles than Bentley's Bike Shop has in stock. How many bicycles does Bentley's Bike Shop have in stock?

_____

7. At Sunflower Bakery's grand opening, the first 250 customers received a free bagel. There were 682 customers at the grand opening. How many customers did not get a free bagel?

_____

8. There were some chairs set up for a concert. Then Shantel set up 256 more chairs. Now 610 chairs are set up. How many chairs were set up to start with?

_____

Mixed Multi-Digit Word Problems

Going Further

▶ Find the Missing Digits

In each box, write the digit that makes a correct addition or subtraction.

1.
```
    ☐ 9
+   8 ☐
-------
  1 2 6
```

2.
```
    8 ☐
-   ☐ 4
-------
    5 7
```

3.
```
    7 ☐
+   ☐ 8
-------
  1 3 0
```

4.
```
  1 ☐ 5
-   4 ☐
-------
    8 6
```

5.
```
    3 ☐ 9
+   ☐ 7 ☐
---------
  1 1 8 5
```

6.
```
    ☐ ☐ 5
+   3 9 ☐
---------
  ☐ 0 2 3
```

7.
```
  5 8 ☐
- ☐ ☐ 6
-------
  4 3 6
```

8.
```
    5 ☐ 7
-   2 6 ☐
---------
    ☐ 4 9
```

9.
```
    ☐ 6 4
+   3 ☐ 8
---------
    9 5 ☐
```

10.
```
  9 ☐ 2 8
- ☐ 1 ☐ 3
---------
  4 8 5 ☐
```

11.
```
    ☐ 7 ☐ 6
+   2 3 8 ☐
-----------
    4 ☐ 4 0
```

12.
```
  6 ☐ 2 ☐
- ☐ 1 ☐ 8
---------
  3 8 2 2
```

➡ 13. On the Back Write your own missing digit addition and missing digit subtraction.

Mixed Multi-Digit Word Problems

Name _____   **Date** _____

Class Activity

▶ Math and Social Studies

1. Find the difference between the height of the Statue of Liberty and the height of your teacher.

   _____

2. The table shows the length of different parts of the Statue of Liberty. Fill in the table. Then find each difference.

111 ft

Length	Statue of Liberty	You	Difference
Pointing Finger	about 96 inches		
Left Hand	about 128 inches		
Right Arm	about 504 inches		

3. **Use a Calculator** There are 168 steps to climb in the Statue of Liberty. Measure how long it takes you to climb a stairway. Use that information to find out how about how long it would take you to climb to the top of the Statue of Liberty. Explain what you did.

   _____

   _____

   _____

   _____

Class Activity

►A Day at the Amusement Park

Pedro's class is going to the amusement park.

The timeline shows how the students will spend their day.

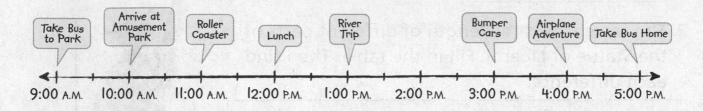

1. What time will Pedro's class go on the Airplane Adventure?

   _____

2. How long is the trip on the bus to the amusement park?

   _____

3. The students went on the Ferris wheel at 3:30 P.M. Mark that on the timeline.

4. Put these events in order starting with the earliest: Airplane Adventure, Roller Coaster, River Trip.

   _____

   _____

5. **Math Journal** Make a timeline that shows how you would like to spend the day at an amusement park. Then write two sentences about your timeline.

Use Mathematical Processes

Name _____ Date _____

Solve each problem. Label your answer.

Show your work.

1. Helga is a dog walker. Today she walked 8 beagles and some terriers. Altogether she walked 14 dogs. How many terriers did she walk?

   _____

2. Li Wei had some apples. She gave 9 of the apples to her friends. She has 5 apples left. How many apples did she start with?

   _____

3. Luis received 6 cards. He received 7 fewer cards than Carlos received. How many cards did Carlos receive?

   _____

4. On Tuesday, Rashid polished 143 rocks. He polished some more rocks on Wednesday. He polished 228 rocks altogether. How many rocks did Rashid polish on Wednesday?

   _____

5. Some students were playing in the schoolyard. Then 119 students went into the school. Now there are 286 students in the schoolyard. How many students were in the schoolyard to start with?

   _____

6. Pat has 425 pennies in his collection. Miguel has 201 fewer pennies. How many pennies does Miguel have?

   _____

7. Write a number to make the number sentence true.

   a. $10 = \boxed{} + 3$ b. $8 - \boxed{} \neq 3$

   c. $5 + \boxed{} = 11$ d. $15 > \boxed{} + 8$

   e. $9 - 2 < \boxed{} + 5$

Write an equation and then solve each problem.
Label your answer.

Show your work.

8. On Monday and Tuesday, Franco spent 5 hours
doing homework altogether. He did homework
for 2 hours on Tuesday. How many hours did
Franco spend doing homework on Monday?

_____

9. Tony had some baseball cards. Jeremy gave him
8 more. Then he had 19 baseball cards. How
many did he have to start?

_____

10. **Extended Response** Elsa read 13 books this month.
She read 6 fewer books than Cliff read.
Draw Comparison Bars to represent the problem.

   How many books did Cliff read? _____

   Explain how you know who read more books,
Elsa or Cliff.

_____

_____

Test

Class Activity

► **Review Quadrilaterals and Types of Lines**

Place the letter Q on each quadrilateral. Then label each quadrilateral with the names that describe it using the letters from the Key.

1.

2.

3.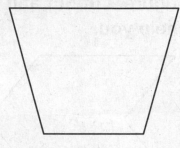

4.

5.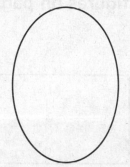

6.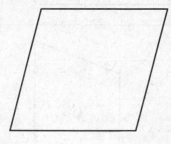

7.

8.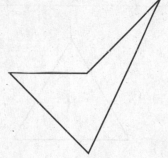

9.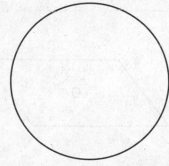

10.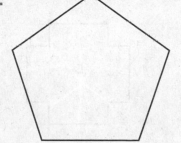

11.

12.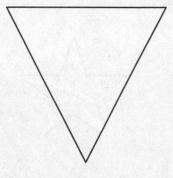

Name _____ **Date** _____

Class Activity

Vocabulary

line of symmetry

▶ Draw Lines of Symmetry

A **line of symmetry** divides a figure in half so that if you fold along the line, the two halves match each other exactly.

Draw all of the possible lines of symmetry on each figure. Cut out and fold the figures on page 101 to help you.

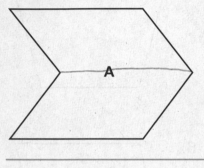

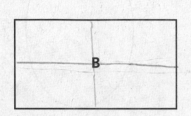

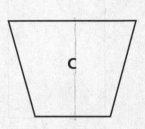

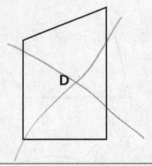

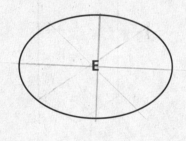

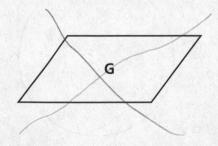

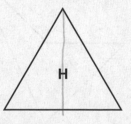

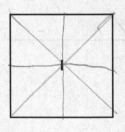

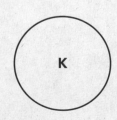

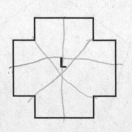

Symmetry and Congruence

Class Activity

Name _____   Date _____

► Draw Lines of Symmetry

Cut out these figures to help you with Student
Activity Book page 98.

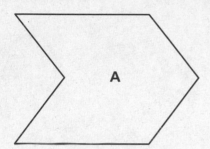

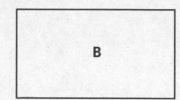

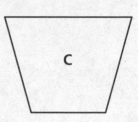

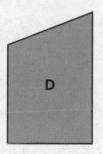

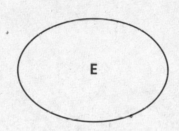

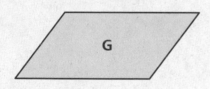

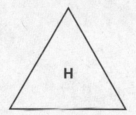

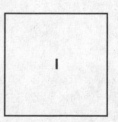

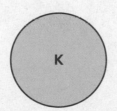

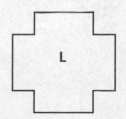

Symmetry and Congruence

Going Further

▶ Use Congruence and Symmetry

Solve.

1. The triangles at the right are congruent. Find the missing measure.

   _____

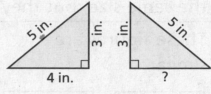

2. Complete the figure so it has the line of symmetry shown.

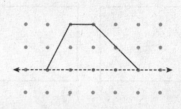

3. All parts of the two dog houses are congruent. How tall is Fido's dog house?

   _____

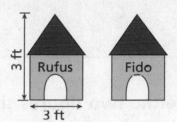

4. The lines of symmetry shown in the figure at the right divide the figure into congruent triangles. The base (short side) of one triangle measures 10 inches. What is the perimeter of the figure?

   _____

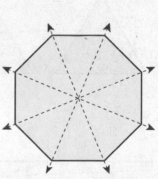

5. The rectangular field at the right has the lines of symmetry shown. How many feet of fencing are needed?

   _____

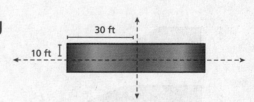

6. **Math Journal** Draw a design that has at least one line of symmetry and that uses at least two congruent figures.

Going Further

Name _____ **Date** _____

► Identify Similar Figures

Similar figures are the same shape. They may also be the same size, but they don't have to be.

These figures are similar.	These figures are similar.	These figures are not similar.

Are the two figures similar? Write similar or not similar.

1.
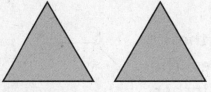

_____

2.
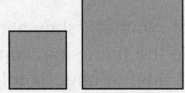

_____

3.

_____

4.
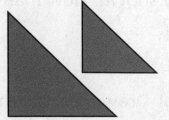

_____

Symmetry and Congruence

Dear Family,

Your child is currently participating in math activities that help him or her understand basic geometry in two dimensions.

Your child will be looking for **lines of symmetry**. If you fold a figure along a line of symmetry, the two halves will match each other exactly.

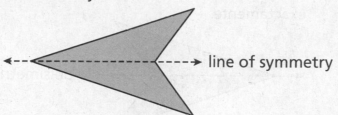 line of symmetry

Your child will also be identifying **congruent** figures. Congruent figures are the same size and shape.

Encourage your child to look for congruent figures in your home or neighborhood and to identify lines of symmetry in various two-dimensional figures.

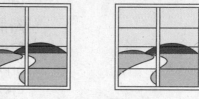

Your child will be learning how to label, name, and describe geometric figures. For example, the line segment *AC* is a **diagonal** of the square *ABCD*.

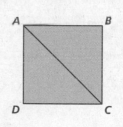

Your child will learn that angles are measured in **degrees** and discover that the sum of the measures of the angles in a triangle is always 180 degrees (180°).

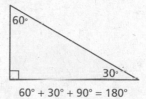

60° + 30° + 90° = 180°

If you have any questions or comments, please call or write to me.

Thank you.

Sincerely,
Your child's teacher

Estimada familia:

En estos momentos su niño o niña está participando en actividades matemáticas que le ayudan a entender la geometria básica en dos dimensiones.

Su niño o niña buscará **ejes de simetría**. Si se pliega una figura a lo largo de su eje de simetría, las dos mitades coincidirán exactamente.

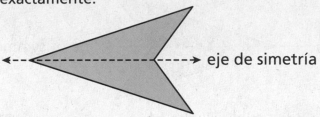
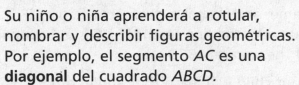 eje de simetría

Su niño o niña también identificará figuras **congruentes**. Las figuras congruentes tienen el mismo tamaño y forma.

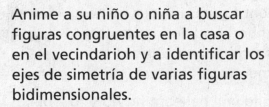

Anime a su niño o niña a buscar figuras congruentes en la casa o en el vecindarioh y a identificar los ejes de simetría de varias figuras bidimensionales.

Su niño o niña aprenderá a rotular, nombrar y describir figuras geométricas. Por ejemplo, el segmento *AC* es una **diagonal** del cuadrado *ABCD*.

Su niño o niña aprenderá que los ángulos se miden en **grados** y descubrirá que la suma de las medidas de los ángulos de un triángulo es siempre 180 grados (180°).

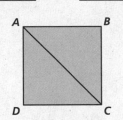
$60° + 30° + 90° = 180°$

Si tiene alguna pregunta o comentario, por favor comuníquese conmigo.

Gracias.

Atentamente,
El maestro de su niño

Symmetry and Congruence

Name

Date

► Label Corners with Letters

You can name figures by labeling their corners with letters.

Give two possible names for each figure.

1.

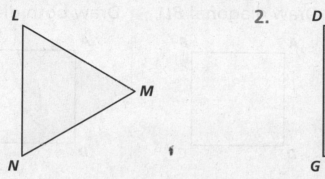

2.

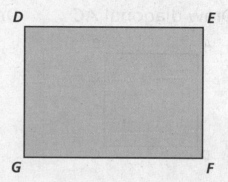

_____

_____

_____

_____

3. Draw a triangle. Name it *ABC*.

4. Draw a rectangle. Name it *MNOP*.

Class Activity

Vocabulary

diagonal

► Diagonals

A line segment that connects two corners of a figure and is not a side is called a **diagonal**.

5. Draw the diagonals in the square.

| Draw diagonal *AC*. | Draw diagonal *BD*. | Draw both diagonals. |

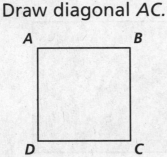 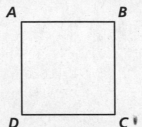 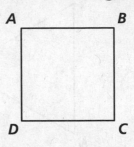

6. What do you notice about the diagonals you drew?

_____

7. What do you notice about the triangles that were formed by the diagonals you drew?

_____

8. Draw the diagonals in the rectangle.

| Draw diagonal *FH*. | Draw diagonal *GI*. | Draw both diagonals. |

9. What do you notice about the diagonals and the triangles they formed?

_____

_____

Label Figures and Draw Diagonals

10. Draw the diagonals in the quadrilateral.

Draw diagonal *WY*.	Draw diagonal *ZX*.	Draw both diagonals.
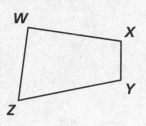	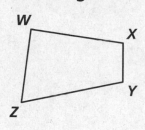	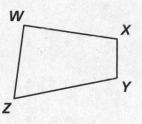

11. What do you notice about the diagonals you drew and the triangles they formed?

_____

_____

12. Draw the diagonals in the parallelogram.

Draw diagonal *KM*.	Draw diagonal *LN*.	Draw both diagonals.
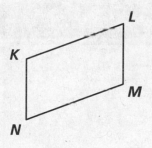	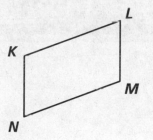	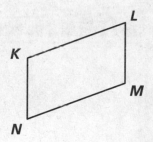

13. What do you notice about the diagonals you drew and the triangles they formed?

_____

_____

14. On the Back Draw a quadrilateral, label it, and draw all the diagonals. Name all of the sides and diagonals of your quadrilateral.

Name

Date

Label Figures and Draw Diagonals

Class Activity

Name   Date

▶ Types of Angles

A **ray** is part of a line that has one endpoint and continues forever in one direction. To draw a ray, make an arrow to show that it goes on forever.

Two line segments or two rays that meet at an endpoint form an **angle**.

An angle that forms a square corner is called a **right angle**.

An angle that is smaller than a right angle is called an **acute angle**.

An angle that is larger than a right angle is called an **obtuse angle**.

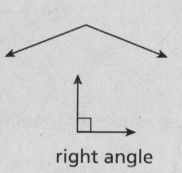

right angle

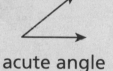

acute angle

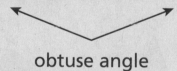

obtuse angle

These angles are named with a letter in the corner.

 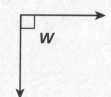 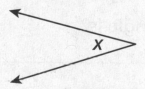 

1. Which of the angles are right angles? _____

2. Which of the angles are acute angles? _____

3. Which of the angles are obtuse angles? _____

Class Activity

Name _____ Date _____

▶ Name Triangles by Sizes of Angles

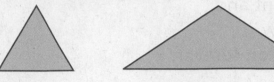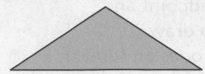

You can name triangles according to the sizes of their angles.

These are **right triangles**.

 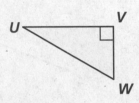 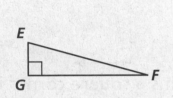 

These are **acute triangles**.

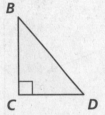 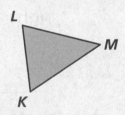 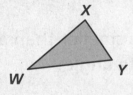

These are **obtuse triangles**.

 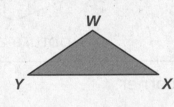  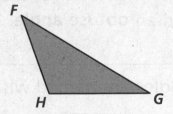

4. What do you think a right triangle is?

_____

5. What do you think an acute triangle is?

_____

6. What do you think an obtuse triangle is?

_____

Angles and Triangles

Class Activity

Name   Date

Vocabulary
equilateral triangle
isosceles triangle
scalene triangle

▶ Name Triangles by Lengths of Sides

You can also name triangles according to the lengths of their sides.

These are **equilateral triangles**.

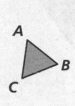
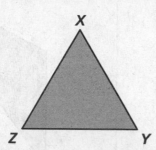
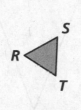
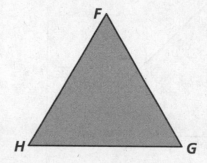

These are **isosceles triangles**.

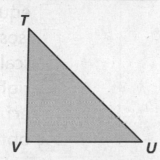
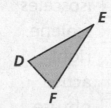
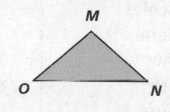

These are **scalene triangles**

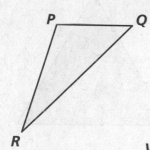
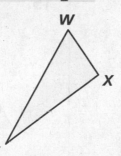
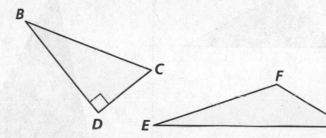

7. What do you think an equilateral triangle is?

_____

8. What do you think an isosceles triangle is?

_____

9. What do you think a scalene triangle is?

► Name Triangles by Sizes of Angles and Lengths of Sides

Mark all the words that describe each triangle.

10.

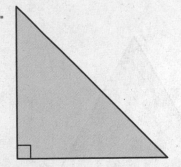

- ☐ equilateral
- ☐ isosceles
- ☐ scalene
- ☐ right
- ☐ acute
- ☐ obtuse

11.

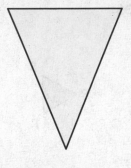

- ☐ equilateral
- ☐ isosceles
- ☐ scalene
- ☐ right
- ☐ acute
- ☐ obtuse

12.

- ☐ equilateral
- ☐ isosceles
- ☐ scalene
- ☐ right
- ☐ acute
- ☐ obtuse

13.

- ☐ equilateral
- ☐ isosceles
- ☐ scalene
- ☐ right
- ☐ acute
- ☐ obtuse

14.

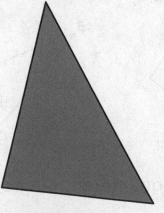

- ☐ equilateral
- ☐ isosceles
- ☐ scalene
- ☐ right
- ☐ acute
- ☐ obtuse

15.

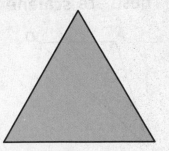

- ☐ equilateral
- ☐ isosceles
- ☐ scalene
- ☐ right
- ☐ acute
- ☐ obtuse

Class Activity

▶ Build Quadrilaterals from Triangles

Cut out each pair of triangles. Use each pair to make as many different quadrilaterals as you can. (You may flip a triangle and use the back.) On a separate piece of paper, trace each quadrilateral that you make.

Obtuse Triangles

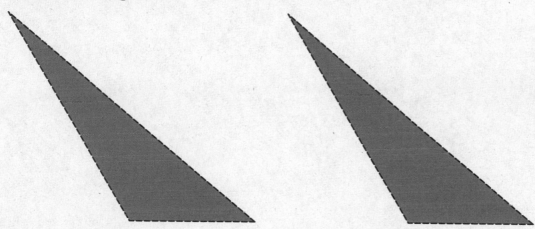

Acute Triangles

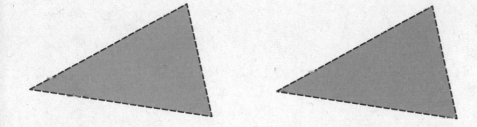

Right Triangles

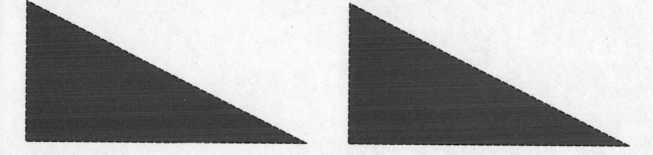

Angles and Triangles

► **Polygons**

A **polygon** is a flat, closed figure made up of line segments that do not cross each other.

Circle the figures that are polygons.

1.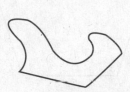

2.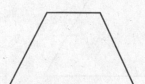

3.

4.

5.

6.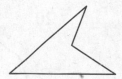

7.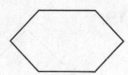

8. (figure)

A figure can be **concave** or **convex**. In concave polygons, there exists a line segment with endpoints inside the polygon and a point on the line segment that is outside the polygon. A convex figure has no such line segment.

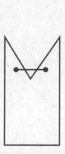 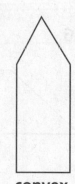

concave   convex

Which figures are convex and which are concave?

9.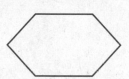

10.

11.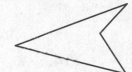

12.

_____   _____   _____   _____

Class Activity

Name   Date

Vocabulary	
pentagon	hexagon
octagon	decagon

► Name Polygons

Polygons are named according to how many sides they have.

3 sides – **tri**angle   4 sides – **quad**rilateral   5 sides – **penta**gon

6 sides – **hexa**gon   8 sides – **octa**gon   10 sides – **deca**gon

Name each figure.

13.

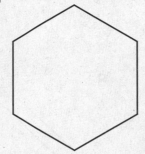

_____

14.

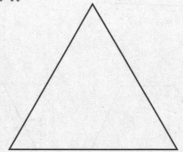

_____

15.

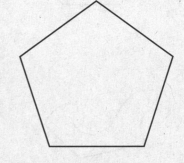

_____

16.

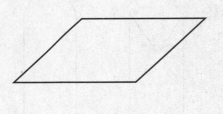

_____

17.

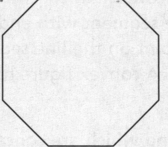

_____

18.

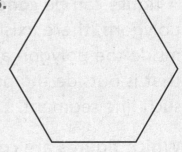

_____

19.

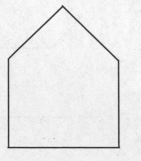

_____

20.

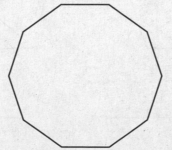

_____

21.

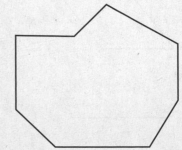

_____

         Angles and Triangles

▶ Build Polygons from Triangles

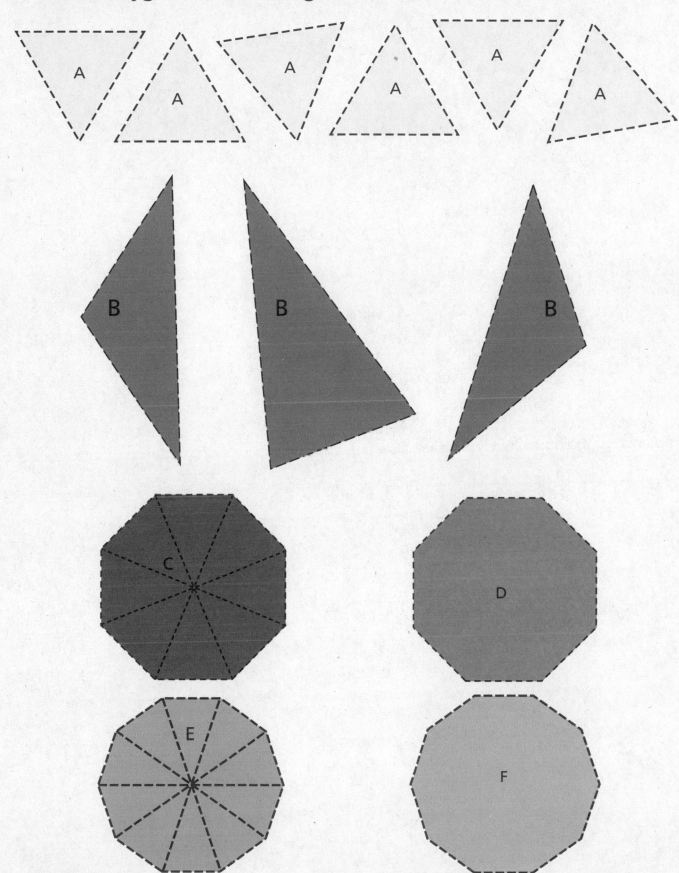

Angles and Triangles

Class Activity

Vocabulary

degree
straight angle
right angle

▶ Introduce Degrees

Angles are measured in units called **degrees**.
One degree is the measure of one very small rotation.

This angle has a measure of 1 degree.

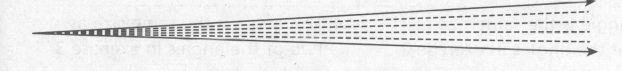

The measure of an angle is the total number of
1-degree angles that fit inside it.

This angle measures 5 degrees.

The symbol for degrees is a small raised circle (°). You
can write the measure of the angle above as 5°.

A **right angle** has a measure of 90°.
A 90°-rotation traces one quarter
of a circle.

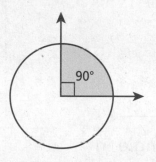

A **straight angle** measures 180°.
A 180°-rotation traces one half of
a circle.

This angle measures 360°.
A 360°-rotation traces a complete
circle.

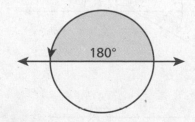

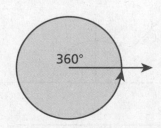

► Angle Measures

Find the size of each angle.

1. This angle is half the size of a right angle.

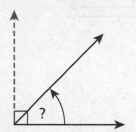

_____

2. If you put three of these angles together, you will get a right angle.

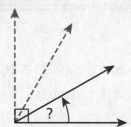

_____

3. This angle is the same size as two of the angles in exercise 2 put together.

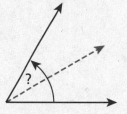

_____

4. This angle is the same size as two of the angles in exercise 3 put together.

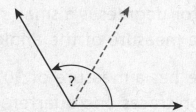

_____

5. This angle is the angle in exercise 1 added to a right angle.

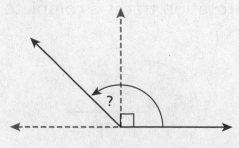

_____

6. This angle is the angle in exercise 2 added to a straight angle.

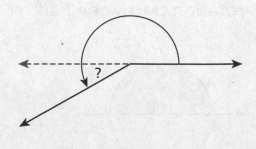

_____

► Join Angles of a Triangle

Draw a large triangle on a sheet of unlined paper. You can draw any type of triangle. Mark each corner with a dot and then cut out the triangle.

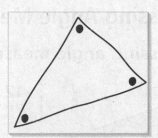

Tear each angle off the triangle, and place the three angles together so that the dotted corners are touching.

7. Sketch your three angles joined at the dotted corners.

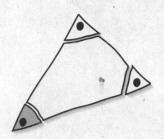

8. What kind of angle is formed when you put together the three angles of your triangle?

_____

Compare your sketch with those of your classmates.

9. Is the sum of the measures of the three angles the same for every triangle?

_____

Complete this statement.

10. The sum of the measures of the three angles in a triangle is _____.

Name _____   **Date** _____

Class Activity

▶ Find Missing Angle Measures

Find the missing angle measure in each triangle.

11.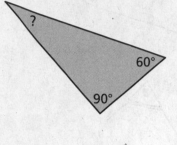

12.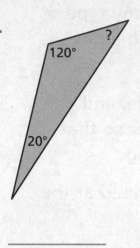

13.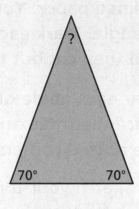

_____   _____   _____

14.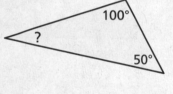

15.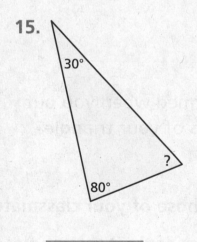

16.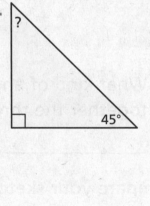

_____   _____   _____

17. In an equilateral triangle, each angle has the same measure. What is the measure of each angle in this equilateral triangle? _____

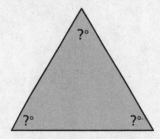

1. Which two figures below are congruent?

Figures _____ and _____ are congruent.

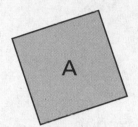

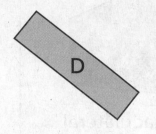

A   B   C   D   E

2. Draw all the lines of symmetry on the figure.

3. Draw diagonal *AC* in the rectangle.

A   B

D   C

Place a check mark next to all of the words that describe the triangle.

4.

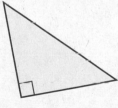

☐ equilateral
☐ isosceles
☐ scalene
☐ right
☐ acute
☐ obtuse

5.

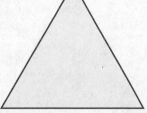

☐ equilateral
☐ isosceles
☐ scalene
☐ right
☐ acute
☐ obtuse

6.

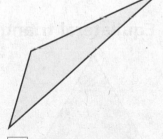

☐ equilateral
☐ isosceles
☐ scalene
☐ right
☐ acute
☐ obtuse

Name _____ **Date** _____

Place a check mark beside the words that describe the figure.

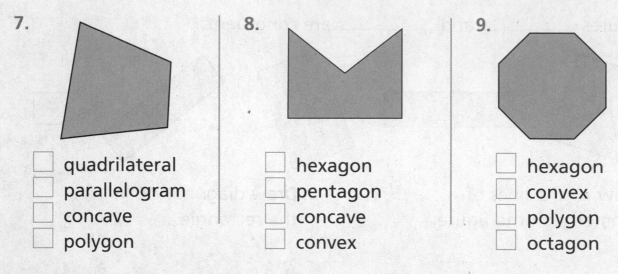

7.

☐ quadrilateral
☐ parallelogram
☐ concave
☐ polygon

8.

☐ hexagon
☐ pentagon
☐ concave
☐ convex

9.

☐ hexagon
☐ convex
☐ polygon
☐ octagon

10. **Extended Response** Trace and cut out each pair of congruent triangles. Make as many quadrilaterals as you can from each pair. Trace the quadrilaterals on a separate sheet of paper. Which pair of triangles makes more quadrilaterals? Explain why.

Isosceles triangles

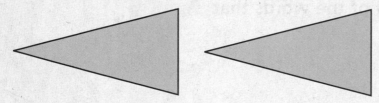

Equilateral triangles

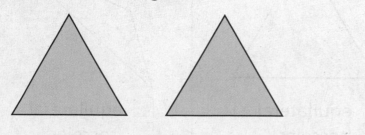

_____

_____

_____

Test

Dear Family,

Your child has started a new unit on using addition and subtraction. These are important math operations that we use almost every day.

At the beginning of the unit, students learn to estimate sums and differences by rounding numbers. They also use estimates to check that actual answers are reasonable, and compare numbers using the symbols for greater than (>), less than (<), or equal to (=).

$$78 > 35 \qquad 114 < 25 + 175 \qquad 14 + 16 = 15 + 15$$

Students also identify and compare the values of a collection of U.S. coins and bills, act out making purchases by counting out the exact amounts, and find out how much change they should receive when giving more than the exact amount for a purchase.

$$66¢ \quad > \quad 41¢$$

Later in the unit, students learn to recognize word problems that contain hidden, extra, and not enough information. They solve problems with two or more steps and learn to analyze information when it is presented in tables and graphs.

Your child is learning how math is used in the world around us. You can help your child learn by sharing shopping situations with them and pointing out graphs and tables in the newspaper or magazines. Encourage your child to spend time acting out shopping situations with coins and bills at home.

Thank you for helping your child learn important math skills.

Sincerely,
Your child's teacher

Carta a la familia

Estimada familia:

Su niño ha comenzado una nueva unidad sobre suma y resta. Éstas son operaciones matemáticas importantes que usamos casi todos los días.

Al principio de esta unidad los estudiantes aprenden a estimar sumas y diferencias redondeando números. También usan la estimación para comprobar que las respuestas que dieron son razonables y comparan números usando los símbolos *mayor que* (>), *menor que* (<) o *igual* (=).

$$78 > 35 \qquad 114 < 25 + 175 \qquad 14 + 16 = 15 + 15$$

Los estudiantes también identifican y comparan los valores de una colección de monedas y billetes de los EE.UU., representan compras contando las cantidades exactas y aprenden cuánto cambio deben recibir cuando dan más de la cantidad exacta durante una compra.

$$66¢ \quad > \quad 41¢$$

Más adelante en esta unidad, los estudiantes aprenden a reconocer problemas verbales que contienen información implícita, exceso o falta de información. Resuelven problemas de dos o más pasos y aprenden a analizar la información presentada en tablas y gráficas.

Su niño está aprendiendo cómo se usan las matemáticas en la vida diaria. Usted puede ayudar a su niño compartiendo situaciones de compra y señalando gráficas y tablas en periódicos o revistas. Anime a su niño a representar en casa situaciones de compra con monedas y billetes.

Gracias por ayudar a su niño a aprender destrezas matemáticas importantes.

Atentamente,
El maestro de su niño

Round to the Nearest Hundred

Name

Date

▶ Coin Equivalents

What relationships do you see in this coin chart?

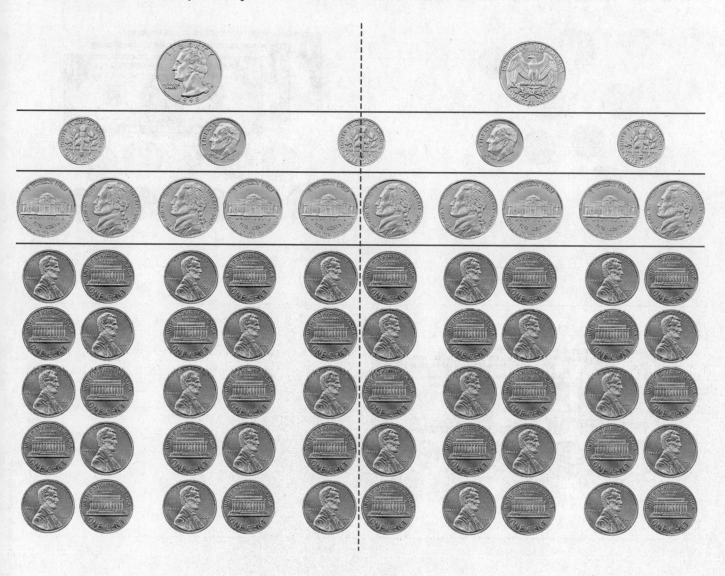

_____

_____

_____

_____

Class Activity

Name _____ **Date** _____

►Count Coins and Bills

Find the value of each collection of coins and bills.

1.

_____

2.

_____

3.

_____

4.

_____

Money Values

Class Activity

▶Compare Amounts of Money

Compare the two collections of coins and bills.
Write >, <, or = in the answer box.

5.

6.

7.

▶Solve Problems Involving Money

Solve each problem.

8. Kevin wants to buy a book that costs $1.50. He has
3 quarters, 6 nickels, and 4 pennies. Does he have
enough money to buy the book?

_____

9. Jade has 7 nickels, 2 dimes, and 5 quarters. Elias
has 8 dimes, 6 pennies, 2 quarters, and 3 nickels.
Who has more money?

_____

➡ 10. On the Back Explain how you solved problem 8.

Money Values

▶ Coins that Make a Dollar

Look at the two different combinations of coins that make a dollar. Can you think of some other coin combinations that make a dollar?

▶ Coin Combinations

Draw two different coin combinations for each amount.

1. 37¢

2. $0.75

Draw each amount with the *fewest* coins. Use quarters, dimes, nickels, or pennies.

3. $0.88

4. $0.43

5. 71¢

6. $.95

These items are for sale at Snappy School Supplies:

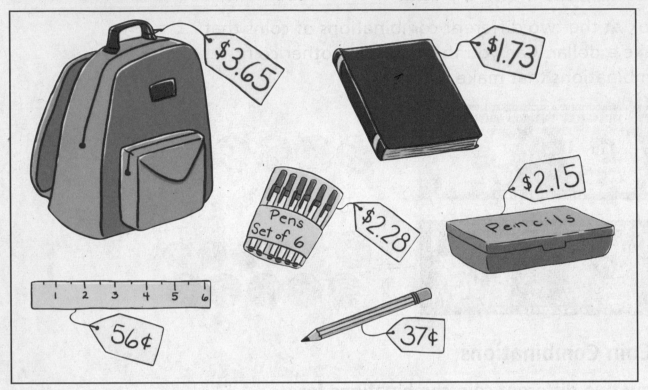

▶ Act It Out

You and your partner can take turns being the customer and the shopkeeper. Here's what to do:

Step 1: The customer chooses two or three items to buy.

Step 2: The shopkeeper writes down the prices and finds the total cost.

Step 3: The customer pays the exact amount of money for the items.

Step 4: The shopkeeper counts the money to make sure it is the right amount and draws the coins and bill used.

Show your work on a separate sheet of paper.

Class Activity

▶Count On to Make Change

Imagine you are working at a sandwich shop. A customer pays for a sandwich that costs $2.78 with a $5 bill. Your cash register is broken and you don't have a pencil. How can you figure out how much change to give the customer?

Start with $2.78. Count on until you get a whole-dollar amount, and then count on by whole dollars until you get to $5.00.

$2.78 $2.79 $2.80 $2.90 $3.00 $4.00 $5.00

Add the coins and bills to find the total amount of change, $2.22.

▶Practice Making Change

Find the amount of change by counting on to the amount paid. Draw the coins and bills you counted.

1. Fernando paid for a $1.39 bottle of juice with two $1 bills. How much change did he get? _____

2. At a garage sale, Ana bought a $3.53 CD with a $5 bill. How much change did she get? _____

3. Valerie bought a $2.12 magazine with three $1 bills. How much change did she get? _____

Name _____ **Date** _____

Class Activity

The following items are for sale at the Beach Snack Shop:

▶Act It Out

You and your partner can take turns being the customer and the shopkeeper. Here's what to do:

Step 1: The customer chooses two items to buy.

Step 2: The shopkeeper writes down the prices and finds the total cost.

Step 3: The customer pays with bills only.

Step 4: The shopkeeper counts on to find the change. Then the shopkeeper writes down the bills used to pay and the amount of change.

Show your work on a separate sheet of paper.

Make Change

►Round Amounts of Money

Round each amount first to the nearest dime and then to the nearest dollar.

	Rounded to the nearest dime	Rounded to the nearest dollar
1. $3.62	_____	_____
2. $5.09	_____	_____
3. $1.25	_____	_____
4. $2.99	_____	_____
5. $7.50	_____	_____

Solve each problem.

Show your work.

6. Carl spent $3.35 on a sandwich and $1.85 on a drink. Estimate the total amount he spent by rounding the prices to the nearest dollar and adding.

_____

7. Rose spent 85¢ on a pen, 32¢ on an eraser, and 78¢ on a pencil sharpener. Estimate the total amount she spent by rounding the prices to the nearest dime and adding.

_____

8. Aisha spent $4.12 on a book, $3.65 on a magazine, and $1.75 on a greeting card. Estimate the total amount she spent by rounding the prices to the nearest dollar and adding.

_____

Class Activity

▶ **Estimate with Money**

Jess brought $5.00 to the store. She wants to buy the items shown at the right. She needs to make an estimate to see if she has enough money.

9. Estimate the total cost of the items by rounding each price to the nearest dollar and adding. Is your estimate $5.00 or less?

_____

10. Find the actual cost of the items. Does Jess have enough money to buy the items?

_____

11. How could Jess make an estimate to be sure she has enough money?

_____

_____

Ben has $3.28. Faiz has $1.63. They want to combine their money to buy a model car that costs $5.00.

12. Estimate the total amount the boys have by rounding each amount to the nearest dollar and adding. Is your estimate $5.00 or more?

_____

13. Find the actual total amount the boys have. Do they have enough to buy the model?

_____

14. How could the boys make an estimate to be sure they have enough money?

_____

_____

Class Activity

Name _____ Date _____

Solve each problem.

Tom's Toy Store

Tang has $1.20. He wants to buy the items shown at the right. He wants to estimate the total cost of the items to make sure he has enough money.

37¢ 12¢ 29¢ 18¢ 10¢

15. How do you think Tang should make his estimate? What estimate do you get if you use your method?

_____

_____

_____

16. Can Tang be sure he has enough money to buy the toys?

_____

_____

Lidia's Garage Sale

Lidia is selling the items shown at the right at a garage sale. She wants to estimate how much money she will make to be sure she will have enough to buy a video game that costs $10.

$2.35 $2.80 $4.75

17. How do you think Lidia should make her estimate? What estimate do you get if you use your method?

_____

_____

_____

18. Can Lidia be sure she will have enough money?

_____

_____

Going Further

▶Different Ways to Estimate with Money

Estimate the total cost of the notebook, marker, and baseball cap using the strategies given below.

Round to the nearest dollar	Use Mental Math
1.	2.

Complete.

3. What is the actual cost of the notebook, marker, and baseball cap? Use your estimates above to check that your answer is reasonable.

_____

4. What estimation strategy would you use to estimate the cost of several items when shopping? Explain.

_____

_____

Round Money Amounts

►Find a Pattern in a Table

Complete the tables and answer the questions.

Blocks in a Tower

Row 1	Row 2	Row 3	Row 4	Row 5	Row 6	Row 7
8 Blocks		6 Blocks	5 Blocks	4 Blocks		

1. What pattern did you use to complete the table?

   _____

Money in Savings Account

Week 1	Week 2	Week 3	Week 4	Week 5	Week 6	Week 7
$300	$285		$255	$240		

2. If the pattern continues, how much money do you predict
   will be in the savings account in week 8? Explain.

   _____

Water Level in Tank

	Hour 1	Hour 2	Hour 3	Hour 4	Hour 5	Hour 6
Tank A	4 in.	5 in.		7 in.	8 in.	
Tank B	6 in.	8 in.	10 in.		14 in.	

3. How would you describe the pattern for each tank?

   _____

   _____

4. **Math Journal** Create your own table with a pattern.
   Describe the pattern.

► **Function Tables**

Vocabulary

function table
rule

Complete each **function table**.

5.

Rule: Add 7	
Input	Output
12	19
25	
32	
54	
68	
73	

6.

Rule: Add 45	
Input	Output
45	90
15	
80	
100	
125	
255	

7.

Rule: Subtract 16	
Input	Output
36	20
48	
88	
100	
126	
159	

Write the **rule** for each function table.

8.

Rule: _____	
Input	Output
20	40
35	55
50	70
65	85
100	120
250	270

9.

Rule: _____	
Input	Output
15	5
20	10
38	28
57	47
110	100
212	202

10.

Rule: _____	
Input	Output
1	16
15	30
40	55
65	80
90	105
120	135

11.

Rule: _____						
Input	100	85	70	65	52	43
Output	95	80	65	60	47	38

Ask Addition and Subtraction Questions from Tables

Class Activity

▶ **Analyze Tables**

This table shows the number of people who went on different rides at an amusement park.

Number of People Who Went on Rides

	Roller Coaster	Ferris Wheel	Bumper Cars
Monday	383	237	185
Tuesday	459	84	348
Wednesday	106	671	215

Use the table above to answer the questions.

1. What do the numbers in the row for Tuesday stand for?

   _____

   _____

   _____

2. What do the numbers in the column for bumper cars stand for?

   _____

   _____

   _____

3. Find the cell with 106 in it. What does this number stand for?

   _____

   _____

Name _____ Date _____

► **Fill in the Tables**

4. This table shows the number of loaves of bread baked and sold last week at the Lotsa Dough Bakery. Fill in the empty cells.

Bread Sales at Lotsa Dough Bakery

	Loaves Baked	Loaves Sold	Loaves Left
Monday	122	38	
Tuesday	113	47	
Wednesday	145		89
Thursday		96	38
Friday	91		44

5. This table shows the number of CDs and videotapes sold at the Sound Out Music Store last week. Fill in the empty cells.

Sound Out Music Sales

	CDs	Videotapes	Total
Monday	62	19	81
Tuesday	73	32	
Wednesday	88		133
Thursday		26	120
Friday	155		223
Saturday		66	294

Going Further

Name _____   Date _____

▶ Use Deductive Reasoning

Solve each problem.

1. Jan, Bev, Luis, and Alex are wearing different color caps. The colors are red, blue, green, and yellow. Jan's cap is not red or green. Alex's cap is red. Bev's cap is not green or yellow. What color cap is each wearing?

	Red	Blue	Green	Yellow
Jan				
Bev				
Luis				
Alex				

_____

_____

2. Ty, Sal, Amy, and Lea were in a race. Amy did not finish either first or second. Lea finished last. Sal finished before Ty. In what order did they finish the race?

	First	Second	Third	Fourth
Ty				
Sal				
Amy				
Lea				

_____

3. Mai, Abdul, Bill, and Rita each play different instruments. The instruments are violin, flute, harp, and guitar. Mai's instrument does not have strings. Bill plays the violin. Abdul does not play the harp. What does each person play?

	violin	flute	harp	guitar
Mai				
Abdul				
Bill				
Rita				

_____

4. **Math Journal** Create your own problem like the ones above.

Name _____ **Date** _____

▶ Use Inductive Reasoning

5. Look for a pattern in the lines of symmetry inside the squares below and the number of triangles formed by them. How many triangles will there be in a square with three lines of symmetry? four lines of symmetry? _____

6. Eight baseball teams will play each of the other teams once. Use a pattern to find how many games will take place? _____

2 teams	3 teams	4 teams	5 teams

1 game	3 games	6 games	10 games

7. Describe the pattern you used to find the answer to Problem 6.

_____

8. Connect the six dots using just three line segments. Do not lift your pencil from the paper or retrace any line segment. The dashed line segments show you a way to start.

9. Connect all nine dots using just four line segments. Do not lift your pencil from the paper or retrace any line segment.

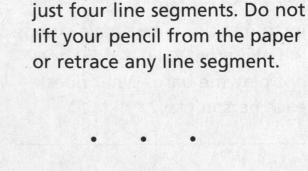

10. Is there a pattern that you could use to solve Problems 8 and 9? _____

Complete Tables

►Make a Table

Use the data the class collected to fill in the table.

►Use a Table

1. Write a comparison question using data from the table above and the word *more.* Answer your question.

_____

_____

2. Write a comparison question using data from the table above and the word *fewer.* Answer your question.

_____

_____

3. Write a question using data from the table and the word *altogether.* Answer your question.

_____

_____

▶Analyze Data

Fill in the missing information in the tables and answer the questions.

This table shows the number of souvenirs the Wildcats baseball team sold last weekend.

Souvenir Sales for Wildcats Baseball Team

	White	Red	Total
Caps	134		211
T-shirts	64	109	
Pennants	59		151

4. Which item above had the most total sales? _____

5. Which color T-shirt had the most sales? _____

This table shows the number of items the Green Thumb Garden Shop sold at their Spring sale.

Spring Sale at Green Thumb Garden Shop

	Number Before the Sale	Number Sold	Number Left
Spades	232	185	
Straw Hats		68	76
Small Pots	412		70
Big Pots		227	98

6. Which item had the most sales? _____

7. Which item has the least number left? _____

More Practice With Tables

▶Solve Problems with Extra Information

Read each problem. Cross out any extra information. Then solve.

1. Emma solved 9 math problems and answered 7 reading questions. Her sister solved 8 math problems. How many math problems did they solve in all?

   _____

2. Mark had 6 shirts and 5 pairs of pants. Today his aunt gave him 4 more shirts and another pair of pants. How many shirts does he have now?

   _____

3. A parking lot had 179 cars and 95 trucks. Then 85 cars left the lot. How many cars are in the parking lot now?

   _____

4. Laura had some roses in a vase. From her garden, she picked 7 more roses and 6 daisies. Now she has 12 roses in all. How many roses did she have at first?

   _____

5. Nikko had 245 pennies and 123 nickels. His brother gave him 89 more pennies and 25 more nickels. How many pennies does Nikko have now?

   _____

▶ Solve Problems with Hidden Information

**Read each problem. Circle the hidden information.
Then solve.**

6. Samuel had 16 horseshoes in the shed yesterday. Today he put a new set of horseshoes on his horse Betsy. How many horseshoes are left in the shed?

_____

7. Maya is going on a vacation with her family for a week and 3 days. How many days will she be on vacation?

_____

8. Julie bought a dozen eggs at the market. She gave 3 of them to Serge. How many eggs does Julie have left?

_____

9. Lisa had 3 quarters and 2 dimes. Then she found 3 nickels and 12 pennies. How many cents does she have now?

_____

10. Marissa is moving away. She is going to move back in a year and 21 days. How many days will she be gone?

_____

Word Problems with Extra or Hidden Information

Name _____ **Date** _____

▶Solve Word Problems with Not Enough Information

Read each problem. Is there a way to solve it? Explain.

1. Sara bought 8 bananas at the fruit market. She put them in a bowl with some oranges. How many pieces of fruit are in the bowl?

_____

_____

2. Josh had some money in his pocket. He spent $1.25 on a bottle of juice. How much money does he have left?

_____

_____

Tell what information is needed to solve each problem.

3. Meg bought 3 mystery books and put them on the shelf with her other mystery books. How many mystery books are now on the shelf?

_____

_____

4. Our school has 5 soccer balls, 6 basketballs, and 4 footballs. Today, some of the footballs were lost. How many balls does the school have now?

_____

_____

Tell what information is needed to solve each problem.

5. A stepladder is 8 feet tall. Two of the steps are broken. How many steps are not broken?

_____

_____

6. Rebecca did 112 dives in competition last summer. This summer, she did many more dives in competition. How many competition dives did she do in the two summers?

_____

_____

7. Today, Maggie's Café sold more hot chocolate than yesterday. Yesterday, Maggie's Café sold 237 cups of hot chocolate. How many more cups were sold today than yesterday?

_____

_____

8. A living room couch is 6 feet long. There are 4 blue pillows and several gray pillows on the couch. How many pillows are on the couch altogether?

_____

_____

Word Problems with Not Enough Information

►Practice

Solve each problem if possible. If more information is needed, rewrite the problem to include the necessary information and then solve it.

9. Leah began fishing at 2 o'clock in the afternoon. She stopped at dinnertime. How many hours did Leah fish?

   _____

   _____

10. On Saturday, Maria handed out 646 flyers in the morning and the same number of flyers in the afternoon. How many flyers did Maria hand out on Saturday?

    _____

    _____

11. The Kitchen Store sold 532 pans and 294 pots. Then some pans were returned. How many pans were not returned?

    _____

    _____

12. There are 3 tables in the room with 4 legs each. One has a broken leg. How many table legs in the room are not broken?

    _____

    _____

▶ Extra Practice

Solve each problem if possible. If more information is needed, rewrite the problem to include the necessary information and then solve it.

13. The train traveled 476 miles on Tuesday. It traveled even more miles on Wednesday. How many miles did the train travel on Tuesday and Wednesday?

_____

_____

14. The hikers walked 12 miles on Tuesday and camped overnight. On Wednesday, they walked back along the same route. How many miles did they hike altogether?

_____

_____

15. One week, Rene cooked meals for 235 people. The next week, she cooked meals for 413 people. How many people did Rene cook meals for in those two weeks?

_____

_____

16. Julio and Scott played 6 card games and 4 computer games today. How many hours did they play games?

_____

_____

► **Solve Two-Step Word Problems**

Show your work.

Solve each problem. Label your answers.

1. The Hillside bus had 14 passengers. When it stopped, 5 people got off and 8 people got on. How many people are riding the Hillside bus now?

_____

2. There are 15 fish in a tank. 12 are goldfish, and the others are angelfish. How many more goldfish are there than angelfish?

_____

3. Luther had 11 sheets of colored paper. 6 were orange, and the rest were blue. Today he used 2 sheets of blue paper. How many sheets of blue paper does Luther have now?

_____

4. Sun Mi picked 14 apricots. Celia picked 5 fewer apricots than Sun Mi. How many apricots did Sun Mi and Celia pick altogether?

_____

5. Annie took 8 photographs at home and 7 photographs at school. Her sister Amanda took 6 fewer photographs than Annie. How many photographs did Amanda take?

_____

Name _____   **Date** _____

Show your work.

▶ Solve and Discuss

Solve each problem. Label your answers.

6. There are 5 mice, 3 gerbils, and some hamsters in a cage. Altogether there are 15 animals in the cage. How many hamsters are there?

_____

7. A new library opened on Saturday. The library lent out 234 books on Saturday. On Sunday, they lent out 138 books. That day, 78 books were returned. How many books were not returned?

_____

8. Katie had 8 dimes and some nickels in her duck bank. She had 4 more nickels than dimes. She took out 5 nickels to buy a newspaper. How many nickels are in her duck bank now?

_____

9. Tony had 14 colored pencils. 9 of them needed sharpening, and the rest were sharp. Yesterday, his uncle gave him some new colored pencils. Now Tony has 12 sharp colored pencils. How many colored pencils did his uncle give him?

_____

10. José ate 6 strawberries. Then he ate 7 more. Lori ate 9 strawberries. How many fewer strawberries did Lori eat than José?

_____

Solve Two-Step Word Problems

▶Solve Multi-Step Word Problems

Show your work.

Solve each problem. Label your answers.

1. Isabel has 14 pieces of fruit. 6 are apples, 2 are bananas, and the rest are pears. Then she buys more pears. Now she has 9 pears. How many pears does she buy?

   _____

2. Four jugglers were practicing. Ted was juggling 3 balls, Ruby was juggling 6 balls, and Mai was juggling 4 balls. 5 of their balls fell. Then Toby started juggling 7 balls. What total number of balls were they juggling then?

   _____

3. Travis had $3.06 and Marie had $1.42. Then Travis earned $1.74 more and Marie earned $2.86 more. Who has more money now? How much more?

   _____

4. Finn delivered 3 pizzas. Then he delivered 5 more pizzas. He delivered 6 fewer pizzas than Liz. How many pizzas did Liz deliver?

   _____

5. Majeed built 7 car models and 14 airplane models. Jasmine built 9 more car models than Majeed and 6 fewer airplane models. How many models did Jasmine build in all?

   _____

▶ Use a Strategy

Read the problem below and answer the questions.

> Marika wants to teach her dog Rufus some tricks. She will reward Rufus with a treat each time he practices a trick. She has a book that lists how many times a dog usually has to practice each trick in order to learn it. The list is shown below.

Trick	Practice Needed
Sit	3 times
Stay	6 times
Fetch	5 times
Come	2 times
Lie down	4 times
Roll over	7 times

6. Marika has 12 treats. She would like to teach Rufus 4 tricks. Can she do it? Explain why or why not.

_____

_____

_____

_____

7. What are all the possible combinations of tricks she can teach with *exactly* 12 treats?

_____

_____

_____

Solve Multi-Step Word Problems

Going Further

▶Use the Work Backward Strategy

Show your work.

Solve each problem. Label your answers.

1. Marvin cut some new line for his fishing pole. Then he cut the new line into 2 equal pieces. Next he cut 8 inches off one piece of line. That gave him a piece of line that was 42 inches long. How long was the original piece of new line?

_____

2. Sam weighed a bag of peanuts. Then he added 2 more pounds of peanuts to the bag. After taking 5 pounds of peanuts out, the bag weighed 6 pounds. How much did the bag of peanuts weigh in the beginning?

_____

3. Tim has a collection of trading cards. His brother gave him 4 more cards. Tim gave 6 cards to his neighbor. Then Tim bought 24 cards. Tim now has 42 cards. How many cards did he have to start with?

_____

4. Jack had an amount of money. He spent $7 for a model car kit and $4 for paint. His mother gave him $5. Jack now has $11. How much money did he have to begin with?

_____

5. **On the Back** Write a word problem that needs to be solved by working backward.

_____

_____

_____

_____

_____

_____

_____

_____

_____

_____

_____

_____

_____

_____

_____

_____

Solve Multi-Step Word Problems

► **Horizontal Bar Graphs with Multi-Digit Numbers**

Use this horizontal bar graph to answer the
questions below.

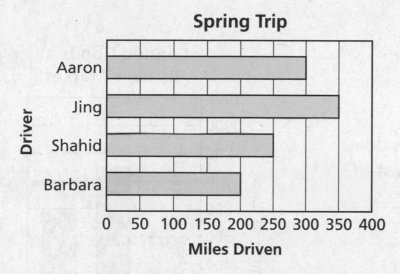

Spring Trip

1. How many miles did Shahid drive?

_____

2. Who drove the most miles?

_____

3. How many miles did Aaron and Barbara drive
   altogether?

_____

4. How many more miles did Jing drive than Shahid?

_____

5. How many fewer miles did Barbara drive than Jing?

_____

6. Write two more questions that can be answered by
   using the graph.

_____

_____

▶Vertical Bar Graphs with Multi-Digit Numbers

Use the vertical bar graph at the right to answer the questions below.

7. How many cans of peas are at Turner's Market?

_____

8. Which type of canned goods does Turner's Market have the least of?

_____

9. How many cans of beans and peaches are there altogether?

_____

10. How many more cans of beans are there than peas?

_____

11. How many fewer cans of peaches are there than peas?

_____

12. Write two more questions that can be answered by using the graph.

_____

_____

_____

_____

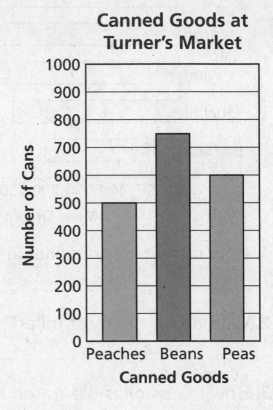

Canned Goods at Turner's Market

Read and Create Bar Graphs with Multi-Digit Numbers

► Create a Horizontal Bar Graph with Multi-Digit Numbers

13. Use the information in this table to make a horizontal bar graph.

Joe's Video Collection	
Type	Videos
Comedy	60
Action	35
Drama	20

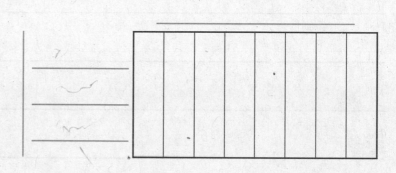

► Create a Vertical Bar Graph with Multi-Digit Numbers

14. Use the information in this table to make a vertical bar graph.

Summer Bike Sales	
Type of Bike	Number Sold
Road Bike	200
Mountain Bike	600
Hybrid Bike	450

15. On the Back Write two questions that can be answered using one of the graphs.

Read and Create Bar Graphs with Multi-Digit Numbers

▶Introduce Frequency Tables and Line Plots

The ages of some players on a basketball team can be shown in different ways.

A **tally chart** can be used to record and organize data.

A **frequency table** shows how many times events occur.

A **line plot** shows the frequency of data on a number line.

Tally Chart	
Age	**Tally**
7	I
8	III
9	ЖI
10	IIII
11	II

Frequency Table	
Age	**Tally**
7	1
8	3
9	5
10	4
11	2

Line Plot

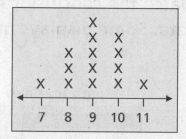

Ages of Basketball Players

▶Review Mode and Range

The **mode** is the value that appears most frequently in a set of data.

The **range** is the difference between the greatest value and the least value in a set of data.

Use the line plot above to complete exercises 1 and 2.

1. What is the mode for the set of data? _____

2. What is the range for the set of data? _____

▶Match Conclusions to Data

Suppose that you work at a toy store. You show information in different displays. Below are conclusions made from displays about toy sales in three stores.

A. Store A sold more items than Store B and Store C.

B. More people bought toys in October than in January.

C. More stuffed animals were sold than any other items.

D. Most dolls purchased cost $10.

Match the conclusions above to the display that represents that data. Some displays may not match a conclusion.

3.

4–Month Toy Sales

October
November
December
January

100 200 300 400
Number of Toys

4.

2008 Toy Sales

Number of Toys Sold

6,000
5,000
4,000
3,000
2,000
1,000

Store A   Store B   Store C
Stores

5.

Prices of Dolls Purchased

	X		
	X		
X	X		
X	X		
X	X		
X	X	X	
X	X	X	X

$5 $10 $15 $20

Price

6.

2008 Toy Sales

Store A 🐻 🐻 🐻 🐻 🐻
Store B 🐻 🐻
Store C 🐻 🐻 🐻 🐻

each 🐻 = 1,000 toys

7.

Weekly Doll Purchases	
Sunday	0
Monday	3
Tuesday	2
Wednesday	3
Thursday	1
Friday	4
Saturday	5

8.

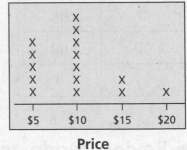

2008 Toy Sales for stores A, B, and C	
Board Games	10,863
Video Games	15,829
Stuffed Animals	29,362
Books	13,256

Represent and Organize Data

Class Activity

► Math and Science

Finish

Three frogs are having a Frog Jumping Contest.
The length of the race is 1,000 cm.
The table shows how far each frog goes in 1 jump.

Name of Frog	Length of Jump
Freddie	about 200 cm
Flora	about 315 cm
Frankie	about 144 cm

Use a Calculator.

1. Bena says it will take Flora about 3 jumps to cross the finish line? Is she right?

   _____

   _____

3. What conclusion can you make about how many of his body lengths Freddie the Frog can jump?

   _____

   _____

2. What conclusions can you make about how many jumps it will take the other frogs to cross the finish line?

   _____

   Freddie's Body Length

   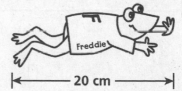

   Freddie

   |←——— 20 cm ———→|

►How Far Can You Jump?

4. Ask 10 students to jump. Measure the length of each jump. Record the names of the students and the length of the jumps in a table.

5. Make a bar graph on grid paper that shows the length of each jump. Put the data in order from shortest jump to longest jump.

6. Look at the graph you made. What is the shape of the data?

_____

7. What is the mode and range?

_____

8. What is your prediction for the jump of another student who has not jumped yet? Why do you think that is a good prediction?

_____

9. What conclusion can you make about how far the 10 students can jump?

_____

_____

Use Mathematical Processes

Compare the numbers. Write >, <, or = in each ◯.

1. 742 ◯ 724

2. 2,329 ◯ 2,319

Write the numbers in order from least to greatest.

3. 598, 678, 590

_____

4. 6,543, 7,585, 6,585

_____

Round each number to the given place.

5. 567 (nearest hundred)

_____

6. $7.89 (nearest dime)

_____

7. $6.29 (nearest dollar)

_____

Use the line plot to answer question 8.

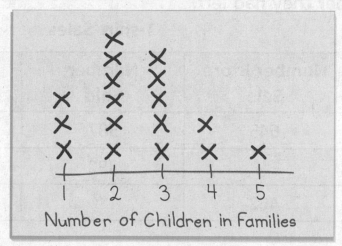

Number of Children in Families

8. What is the mode and range of the data?

mode: _____ range: _____

Use the bar graph to answer questions 9 and 10.

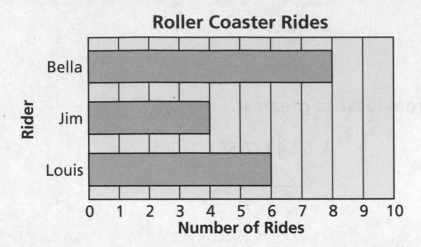

Roller Coaster Rides

9. How many more rides did Louis take than Jim? _____

10. How many rides did Bella and Louis take altogether? _____

This table shows the numbers of T-shirts of different sizes a store had before a big sale, the number they sold, and the number they had left.

T-shirt Sales

	Number Bfore Sale	Number Sold	Number Left After Sale
Small	645	587	
Medium		390	45
Large	462		29

11. Fill in the blank cells.

12. How many more small T-shirts than large T-shirts did the store have before the sale?

_____

Solve. Cross out any extra information. Circle any hidden information.

Show your work.

13. Becky has 20 fish and 2 hamsters. There are 8 angelfish and the rest of the fish are goldfish. She gets 7 more goldfish. How many goldfish does she have now?

_____

14. Raj is going on vacation for a week and 5 days. How many days will Raj be gone?

_____

Solve. Label your answer.

15. Jason has 485 toy dinosaurs in his collection. He plans to sell 243 toy dinosaurs. Round each number to the nearest ten to estimate how many he will have left.

_____

Solve the problem if possible. If more information is needed, rewrite the problem to include the necessary information and then solve it.

16. Julie and Sam grew tomato plants. Julie's plant grew 16 inches. How much taller did Sam's plant grow?

_____

_____

_____

Compare the two collections of coins and bills.
Write >, <, or = in the ⬭.

17.

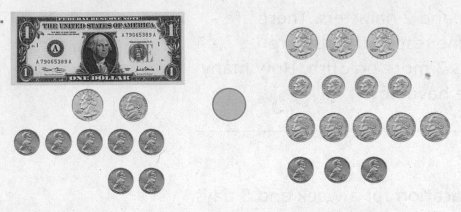

18. Draw two different coin combinations for 78¢.

Solve.

19. Uri bought a tube of toothpaste for $2.58. He paid with a $5.00 bill. Find the amount of change by counting on. Draw the coins and bills you counted. How much change did he get?

Show your work.

_____

20. **Extended Response** Alexa has $5.00. She wants to order a sandwich for $3.65 and a drink for $1.48. How can she estimate to be sure she has enough money? _____

_____

_____

_____

What estimate do you get using your method? Can Alexa be sure she has enough money to buy the sandwich and the drink?

_____

Test

Class Activity

Name _____

Date _____

Vocabulary

flip

▶ Draw Flips

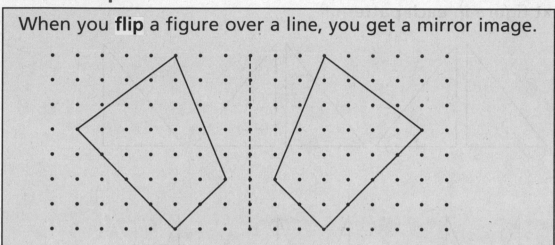

When you **flip** a figure over a line, you get a mirror image.

Draw the flipped image of each figure.

1.

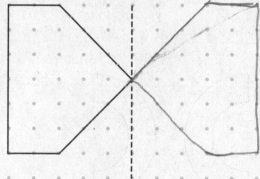

2.

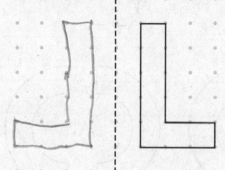

3.

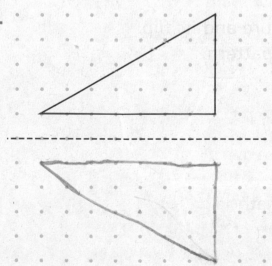

4.

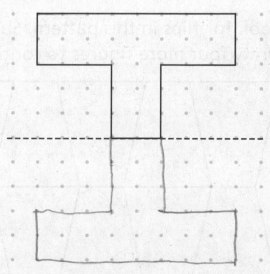

Class Activity

► Use Flips in Patterns

Draw the next figure in each pattern.

5.

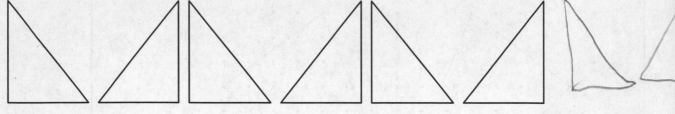

6.

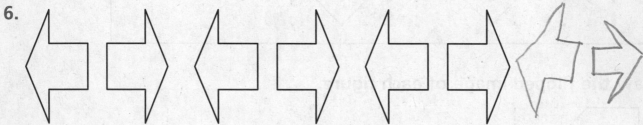

7.

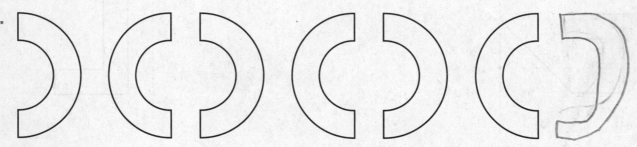

8. Look for flips in this pattern. Shade a figure and its flip. Draw four more figures to continue the pattern.

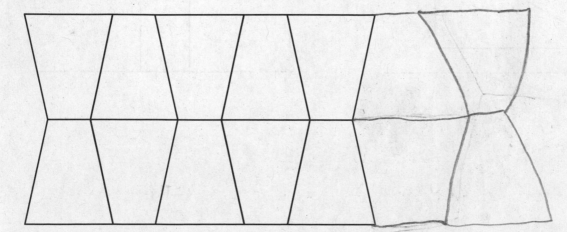

Class Activity

▶ **Describe and Draw Slides**

You can **slide** a figure along a line.

This slide moves the figure to the right and down.

This slide moves the figure up and to the right.

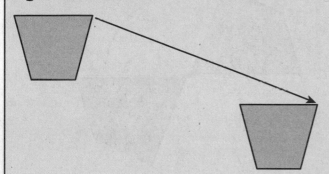

Describe each slide. Draw the new figure.

9.

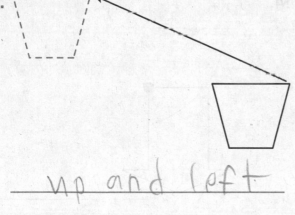

up and left

10.

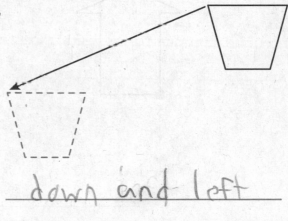

down and left

11.

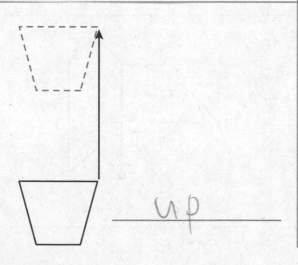

up

12.

left

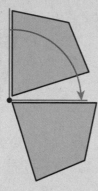

6–1

Class Activity

Name _____

Date _____

Vocabulary

turn

▶ Describe and Draw Turns

You can **turn** a figure around a point.

This is a quarter turn.   This is a half turn.

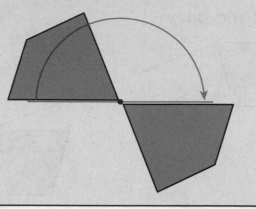

Describe each turn. Draw the new figure.

13.

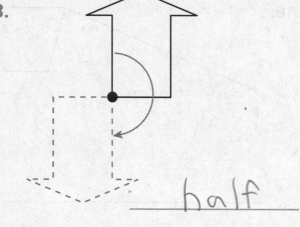

half

14.

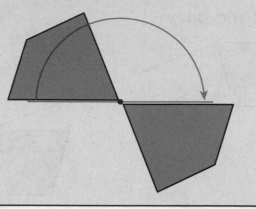

quarter

15.

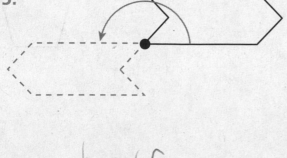

half

16.

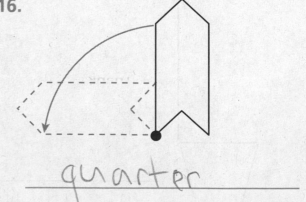

quarter

Motion Geometry Patterns

Dear Family,

Your child is studying patterns that grow, patterns that shrink, and patterns that repeat. Students will find pattern rules and continue patterns for both number and geometric patterns. Students will also use patterns to solve real-world problems. Repeating patterns from geometry are used everywhere: in art, tiling designs, quilts, and clothing. Slides (translations), flips (reflections), and turns (rotations) can be used to make tiling patterns.

This diagram shows how copies of this geometric figure can fit together to make a tiling pattern.

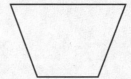

Turn the figure
around a point.

Flip the figure
over a line.

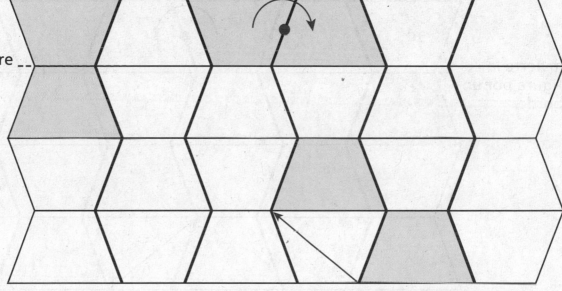

Slide the figure up
and to the left.

If you have any questions or comments, please call or write to me.

Thank you.

Sincerely,
Your child's teacher

Estimada familia:

La unidad que su niño está estudiando trata de patrones: patrones que aumentan, patrones que disminuyen, patrones que se repiten. Los patrones geométricos que se repiten se usan en todas partes: en arte, en diseños de azulejos, en colchas y en ropa. Los deslizamientos (traslaciones), las inversiones (reflexiones) y los giros (rotaciones), servirán para hacer patrones de azulejos.

Este diagrama muestra de qué manera pueden combinarse las copias de esta figura geométrica para formar un patrón de azulejos.

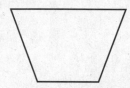

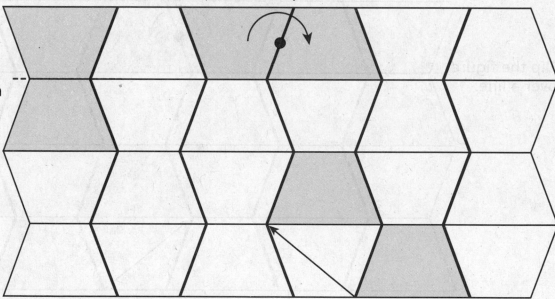

Gira la figura sobre un punto.

Invierte la figura por un borde.

Desliza la figura hacia arriba y la izquierda.

Si tiene alguna pregunta o comentario, por favor comuníquese conmigo. Gracias.

Atentamente,
El maestro de su niño.

Motion Geometry Patterns

Unit Test

1. Is the second figure the result of a slide, flip, or turn?

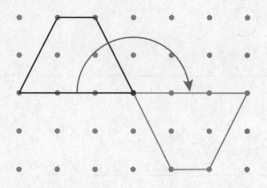

_____

2. Draw the next figure in the pattern.

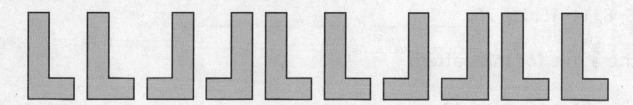

3. Continue the number pattern.

329329329329329 _____

4. Draw the next figure in the pattern.

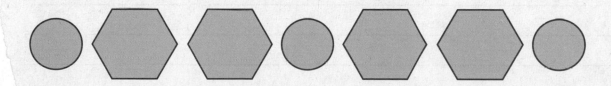

5. Write a rule for this pattern.

_____

6. Continue this pattern.

65, 62, 59, 56, 53, 50, 47, ____ , ____ , ____ , ____ , ____

7. Continue this pattern.

12, 16, 20, 24, 28, 32, 36, ____ , ____ , ____ , ____ , ____

8. Continue this pattern.

5, 6, 8, 11, 15, 20, 26, ____ , ____ , ____ , ____ , ____

9. Write a rule for this pattern.

69, 64, 59, 54, 49, 44, 39

_____

10. Extended Response In September, Elisa walks dogs for $1.25 per walk. In October, she charges $1.50 per walk. In November, she charges $1.75 per walk. If the pattern continues, how much will she charge per walk in December and January? Describe the pattern rule you used to solve the problem.

_____

_____

_____

Dear Family,

In this unit and the next, your child will be practicing basic multiplications and divisions. *Math Expressions* incorporates studying, practicing, and testing of the basic multiplications and divisions in class. Your child is also expected to practice at home.

Study Plans Each day your child will fill out a study plan, indicating which basic multiplications and divisions he or she will study that evening. When your child has finished studying (practicing), his or her Homework Helper should sign the study plan.

4–1	Name		Date
Homework			

Study Plan

5s count bys
5s multiplications

Homework Helper

Practice Charts Each time a new number is introduced, students' homework will include a practice chart. To practice, students can cover the products with a pencil or a strip of heavy paper. They will say the multiplications, sliding the pencil or paper down the column to see each product after saying it. Students can also start with the last problem in a column and slide up. It is important that your child studies count-bys and multiplications at least 5 minutes every night. Your child can also use these charts to practice division on the mixed up column by covering the first factor.

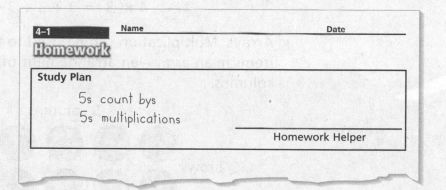

	In Order	Mixed Up
	$1 \times 5 = 5$	$9 \times 5 = 45$
	$2 \times 5 = 10$	$5 \times 5 = 25$
	$3 \times 5 = 15$	$2 \times 5 = 10$
	$4 \times 5 = 20$	$7 \times 5 = 35$
5s	$5 \times 5 = 25$	$4 \times 5 = 20$
	$6 \times 5 = 30$	$6 \times 5 = 30$
	$7 \times 5 = 35$	$10 \times 5 = 50$
	$8 \times 5 = 40$	$8 \times 5 = 40$
	$9 \times 5 = 45$	$1 \times 5 = 5$
	$10 \times 5 = 50$	$3 \times 5 = 15$

To help students understand the concept of multiplication, the *Math Expressions* program presents three ways to think about multiplication. They are described on the back of this letter.

- **Repeated groups:** Multiplication can be used to find the total in repeated groups of the same size. In early lessons, students circle the group size in repeated-groups equations to help keep track of which factor is the group size and which is the number of groups.

4 groups of bananas

$4 \times ③ = 3 + 3 + 3 + 3 = 12$

- **Arrays:** Multiplication can be used to find the total number of items in an *array*—an arrangement of objects into rows and columns.

5 columns

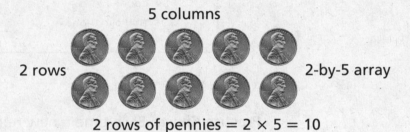

2 rows

2-by-5 array

2 rows of pennies = $2 \times 5 = 10$

- **Area:** Multiplication can be used to find the area of a rectangle.

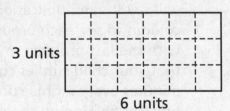

3 units

6 units

Area: 3 units $\times$ 6 units = 18 square units

Please call if you have any questions or comments.

Thank you.

Sincerely,
Your child's teacher

Multiply with 5

Estimada familia:

En esta unidad y la unidad que sigue, su niño va a practicar las multiplicaciones y divisiones básicas. *Math Expressions* incorpora en la clase el estudio, la práctica y la evaluación de las multiplicaciones y divisiones básicas. También se espera que su niño practique en casa.

Planes de estudio Todos los días su niño va a completar un plan de estudio, que indica cuáles multiplicaciones y divisiones debe estudiar esa noche. Cuando su niño haya terminado de estudiar (practicar), la persona que lo ayude debe firmar el plan de estudio.

4–1	Name		Date
Homework			
Study Plan			
5s count bys			
5s multiplications			
			Homework Helper

Tablas de práctica Cada vez que se presente un número nuevo, la tarea de los estudiantes incluirá una tabla de práctica. Para practicar, los estudiantes pueden cubrir los productos con un lápiz o una tira de papel grueso. Los niños dicen la multiplicación y deslizan el lápiz o el papel hacia abajo para revelar el producto después de decirlo. También pueden empezar con el último problema de la columna y deslizar el lápiz o el papel hacia arriba. Es importante que su niño practique el conteo y la multiplicación por lo menos 5 minutos cada noche. Su niño también puede usar estas tablas para practicar la división en la columna de productos desordenados cubriendo el primer factor.

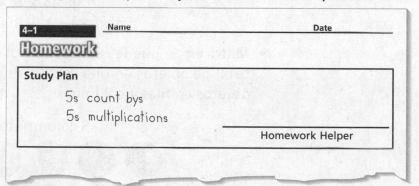

En orden	Desordenados
1 × 5 = 5	9 × 5 = 45
2 × 5 = 10	5 × 5 = 25
3 × 5 = 15	2 × 5 = 10
4 × 5 = 20	7 × 5 = 35
5 × 5 = 25	4 × 5 = 20
6 × 5 = 30	6 × 5 = 30
7 × 5 = 35	10 × 5 = 50
8 × 5 = 40	8 × 5 = 40
9 × 5 = 45	1 × 5 = 5
10 × 5 = 50	3 × 5 = 15

(Columna izquierda con el número **5**)

Para ayudar a los estudiantes a comprender el concepto de la multiplicación, el programa *Math Expressions* presenta tres maneras de pensar en la multiplicación. Éstas se describen a continuación.

- **Grupos repetidos:** La multiplicación se puede usar para hallar el total con grupos del mismo tamaño que se repiten. Cuando empiezan a trabajar con ecuaciones de grupos repetidos, los estudiantes rodean con un círculo el tamaño del grupo en las ecuaciones, para recordar cuál factor representa el tamaño del grupo y cuál representa el número de grupos.

4 grupos de bananas

$4 \times ③ = 3 + 3 + 3 + 3 = 12$

- **Matrices:** Se puede usar la multiplicación para hallar el número total de objetos en una *matriz,* es decir, una disposición de objetos en filas y columnas.

5 columnas

2 filas   matriz de 2 por 5

2 filas de monedas de un centavo = $2 \times 5 = 10$

- **Área:** Se puede usar la multiplicación para hallar el área de un rectángulo.

3 unidades

6 unidades

Área: 3 unidades $\times$ 6 unidades = 18 unidades cuadradas

Si tiene alguna duda o comentario, por favor comuníquese conmigo. Gracias.

Atentamente,
El maestro de su niño

Multiply with 5

Name _____ Date _____

Signature Sheet

	Count-Bys Partner	Multiplications Partner	Divisions Partner	Multiplications Sprint	Divisions Sprint
0					
1					
2					
3					
4					
5					
6					
7					
8					
9					
10					

Signature Sheet

Study Sheet A

2s

Count-bys	Mixed Up ×	Mixed Up ÷
$1 \times 2 = 2$	$7 \times 2 = 14$	$20 \div 2 = 10$
$2 \times 2 = 4$	$1 \times 2 = 2$	$2 \div 2 = 1$
$3 \times 2 = 6$	$3 \times 2 = 6$	$6 \div 2 = 3$
$4 \times 2 = 8$	$5 \times 2 = 10$	$16 \div 2 = 8$
$5 \times 2 = 10$	$6 \times 2 = 12$	$12 \div 2 = 6$
$6 \times 2 = 12$	$8 \times 2 = 16$	$4 \div 2 = 2$
$7 \times 2 = 14$	$2 \times 2 = 4$	$10 \div 2 = 5$
$8 \times 2 = 16$	$10 \times 2 = 20$	$8 \div 2 = 4$
$9 \times 2 = 18$	$4 \times 2 = 8$	$14 \div 2 = 7$
$10 \times 2 = 20$	$9 \times 2 = 18$	$18 \div 2 = 9$

9s

Count-bys	Mixed Up ×	Mixed Up ÷
$1 \times 9 = 9$	$2 \times 9 = 18$	$81 \div 9 = 9$
$2 \times 9 = 18$	$4 \times 9 = 36$	$18 \div 9 = 2$
$3 \times 9 = 27$	$7 \times 9 = 63$	$36 \div 9 = 4$
$4 \times 9 = 36$	$8 \times 9 = 72$	$9 \div 9 = 1$
$5 \times 9 = 45$	$3 \times 9 = 27$	$54 \div 9 = 6$
$6 \times 9 = 54$	$10 \times 9 = 90$	$27 \div 9 = 3$
$7 \times 9 = 63$	$1 \times 9 = 9$	$63 \div 9 = 7$
$8 \times 9 = 72$	$6 \times 9 = 54$	$72 \div 9 = 8$
$9 \times 9 = 81$	$5 \times 9 = 45$	$90 \div 9 = 10$
$10 \times 9 = 90$	$9 \times 9 = 81$	$45 \div 9 = 5$

5s

Count-bys	Mixed Up ×	Mixed Up ÷
$1 \times 5 = 5$	$2 \times 5 = 10$	$10 \div 5 = 2$
$2 \times 5 = 10$	$9 \times 5 = 45$	$35 \div 5 = 7$
$3 \times 5 = 15$	$1 \times 5 = 5$	$50 \div 5 = 10$
$4 \times 5 = 20$	$5 \times 5 = 25$	$5 \div 5 = 1$
$5 \times 5 = 25$	$7 \times 5 = 35$	$20 \div 5 = 4$
$6 \times 5 = 30$	$3 \times 5 = 15$	$15 \div 5 = 3$
$7 \times 5 = 35$	$10 \times 5 = 50$	$30 \div 5 = 6$
$8 \times 5 = 40$	$6 \times 5 = 30$	$40 \div 5 = 8$
$9 \times 5 = 45$	$4 \times 5 = 20$	$25 \div 5 = 5$
$10 \times 5 = 50$	$8 \times 5 = 40$	$45 \div 5 = 9$

10s

Count-bys	Mixed Up ×	Mixed Up ÷
$1 \times 10 = 10$	$1 \times 10 = 10$	$80 \div 10 = 8$
$2 \times 10 = 20$	$5 \times 10 = 50$	$10 \div 10 = 1$
$3 \times 10 = 30$	$2 \times 10 = 20$	$50 \div 10 = 5$
$4 \times 10 = 40$	$8 \times 10 = 80$	$90 \div 10 = 9$
$5 \times 10 = 50$	$7 \times 10 = 70$	$40 \div 10 = 4$
$6 \times 10 = 60$	$3 \times 10 = 30$	$100 \div 10 = 10$
$7 \times 10 = 70$	$4 \times 10 = 40$	$30 \div 10 = 3$
$8 \times 10 = 80$	$6 \times 10 = 60$	$20 \div 10 = 2$
$9 \times 10 = 90$	$10 \times 10 = 100$	$70 \div 10 = 7$
$10 \times 10 = 100$	$9 \times 10 = 90$	$60 \div 10 = 6$

208 UNIT 7 LESSON 3

Copyright © Houghton Mifflin Company. All rights reserved.

Study Sheet A

Dear Family,

In addition to practice charts for the basic multiplications and divisions for each of the numbers 1 through 10, your child will bring home a variety of other practice materials over the next several weeks.

- **Home Study Sheets:** A Home Study Sheet includes 3 or 4 practice charts on one page. Your child can use the Home Study Sheets to practice all the count-bys, multiplications, and divisions for a number or to practice just the ones he or she doesn't know for that number. The Homework Helper can then use the sheet to test (or retest) your child. The Homework Helper should check with your child to see which basic multiplications or divisions he or she is ready to be tested on. The helper should mark any missed problems lightly with a pencil.

  If your child gets all the answers in a column correct, the helper should sign that column on the Home Signature Sheet. When signatures are on all the columns of the Home Signature Sheet, your child should bring the sheet to school.

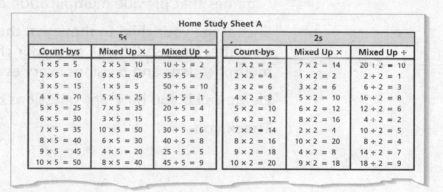

Home Study Sheet A

5s			2s		
Count-bys	Mixed Up ×	Mixed Up ÷	Count-bys	Mixed Up ×	Mixed Up ÷
1 × 5 = 5	2 × 5 = 10	10 ÷ 5 = 2	1 × 2 = 2	7 × 2 = 14	20 ÷ 2 = 10
2 × 5 = 10	9 × 5 = 45	35 ÷ 5 = 7	2 × 2 = 4	1 × 2 = 2	2 ÷ 2 = 1
3 × 5 = 15	1 × 5 = 5	50 ÷ 5 = 10	3 × 2 = 6	3 × 2 = 6	6 ÷ 2 = 3
4 × 5 = 20	5 × 5 = 25	5 ÷ 5 = 1	4 × 2 = 8	5 × 2 = 10	16 ÷ 2 = 8
5 × 5 = 25	7 × 5 = 35	20 ÷ 5 = 4	5 × 2 = 10	6 × 2 = 12	12 ÷ 2 = 6
6 × 5 = 30	3 × 5 = 15	15 ÷ 5 = 3	6 × 2 = 12	8 × 2 = 16	4 ÷ 2 = 2
7 × 5 = 35	10 × 5 = 50	30 ÷ 5 = 6	7 × 2 = 14	2 × 2 = 4	10 ÷ 2 = 5
8 × 5 = 40	6 × 5 = 30	40 ÷ 5 = 8	8 × 2 = 16	10 × 2 = 20	8 ÷ 2 = 4
9 × 5 = 45	4 × 5 = 20	25 ÷ 5 = 5	9 × 2 = 18	4 × 2 = 8	14 ÷ 2 = 7
10 × 5 = 50	8 × 5 = 40	45 ÷ 5 = 9	10 × 2 = 20	9 × 2 = 18	18 ÷ 2 = 9

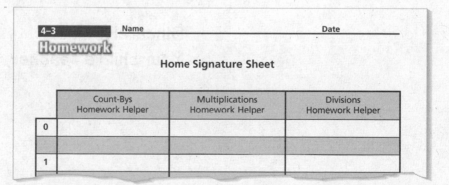

4–3

Homework

Name _____ Date _____

Home Signature Sheet

	Count-Bys Homework Helper	Multiplications Homework Helper	Divisions Homework Helper
0			
1			

- **Home Check Sheets:** A Home Check Sheet includes columns of 20 multiplications and divisions in mixed order. These sheets can be used as a more challenging alternative to the Home Study Sheets.

- **Strategy Cards:** Students use Strategy Cards in class as flashcards, to play games, and to develop multiplication and division strategies.

Sample Multiplication Card

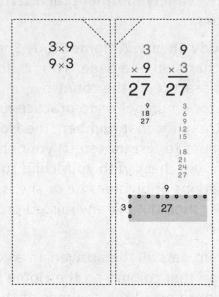

Sample Division Card

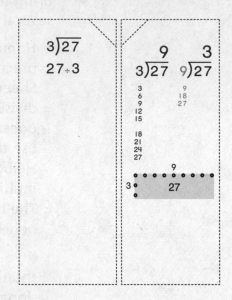

- **Games:** Near the end of this unit, students are introduced to games that provide multiplication and division practice.

Encourage your child to show you these materials and explain how they are used. Make sure your child spends time practicing multiplications and divisions every evening.

Please call if you have any questions or comments.

Thank you.

Sincerely,
Your child's teacher

Multiplication and Arrays

Estimada familia:

Además de las tablas de práctica para las multiplicaciones y divisiones básicas para cada número del 1 al 10, su niño llevará a casa una variedad de materiales de práctica en las semanas que vienen.

- **Hojas para estudiar en casa:** Una hoja para estudiar en casa incluye 3 ó 4 tablas de práctica en una página. Su niño puede usar las hojas para practicar todos los conteos, multiplicaciones y divisiones de un número, o para practicar sólo las operaciones para ese número que no domine. La persona que ayude a su niño con la tarea puede usar la hoja para hacerle una prueba (o repetir una prueba). Esa persona debe hablar con su niño para decidir sobre qué multiplicaciones o divisiones básicas el niño puede hacer la prueba. La persona que ayude debe marcar ligeramente con un lápiz cualquier problema que conteste mal. Si su niño contesta bien todas las operaciones de una columna, la persona que ayude debe firmar esa columna de la hoja de firmas. Cuando todas las columnas de la hoja de firmas estén firmadas, su niño debe llevar la hoja a la escuela.

Home Study Sheet A

5s			2s		
Count-bys	Mixed Up ×	Mixed Up ÷	Count-bys	Mixed Up ×	Mixed Up ÷
1 × 5 = 5	2 × 5 = 10	10 ÷ 5 = 2	1 × 2 = 2	7 × 2 = 14	20 ÷ 2 = 10
2 × 5 = 10	9 × 5 = 45	35 ÷ 5 = 7	2 × 2 = 4	1 × 2 = 2	2 ÷ 2 = 1
3 × 5 = 15	1 × 5 = 5	50 ÷ 5 = 10	3 × 2 = 6	3 × 2 = 6	6 ÷ 2 = 3
4 × 5 = 20	5 × 5 = 25	5 ÷ 5 = 1	4 × 2 = 8	5 × 2 = 10	16 ÷ 2 = 8
5 × 5 = 25	7 × 5 = 35	20 ÷ 5 = 4	5 × 2 = 10	6 × 2 = 12	12 ÷ 2 = 6
6 × 5 = 30	3 × 5 = 15	15 ÷ 5 = 3	6 × 2 = 12	8 × 2 = 16	4 ÷ 2 = 2
7 × 5 = 35	10 × 5 = 50	30 ÷ 5 = 6	7 × 2 = 14	2 × 2 = 4	10 ÷ 2 = 5
8 × 5 = 40	6 × 5 = 30	40 ÷ 5 = 8	8 × 2 = 16	10 × 2 = 20	8 ÷ 2 = 4
9 × 5 = 45	4 × 5 = 20	25 ÷ 5 = 5	9 × 2 = 18	4 × 2 = 8	14 ÷ 2 = 7
10 × 5 = 50	8 × 5 = 40	45 ÷ 5 = 9	10 × 2 = 20	9 × 2 = 18	18 ÷ 2 = 9

4–3
Homework

Name _____   Date _____

Home Signature Sheet

	Count-Bys Homework Helper	Multiplications Homework Helper	Divisions Homework Helper
0			
1			

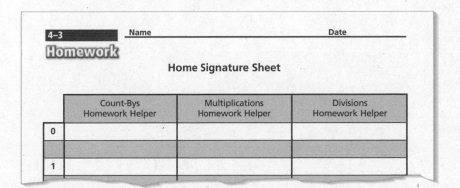

- **Hojas de verificación:** Una hoja de verificación consta de columnas de 20 multiplicaciones y divisiones sin orden fijo. Estas hojas pueden usarse como alternativa de mayor desafío que las hojas para estudiar en casa.

CARTA A LA FAMILIA

- **Tarjetas de estrategias:** Los estudiantes usan las tarjetas de estrategias en la clase como ayuda de memoria, en juegos y para desarrollar estrategias para hacer multiplicaciones y divisións.

Ejemplo de tarjeta de multiplicación   **Ejemplo de tarjeta de división**

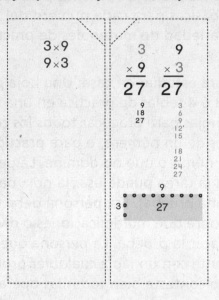 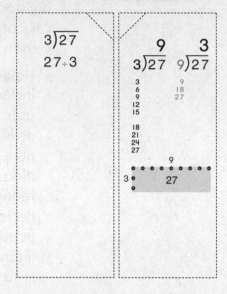

- **Juegos:** Hacia el final de esta unidad se les presentan a los estudiantes juegos para practicar la multiplicación y la división.

Anime a su niño a que le muestre a Ud. estos materiales y a que le explique cómo se usan. Asegúrese de que su niño practique la multiplicación y la división cada noche.

Si tiene alguna duda o pregunta, por favor comuníquese conmigo.

Atentamente,
El maestro de su niño

Multiplication and Arrays

Class Activity

▶ Explore Division

Solve each problem.

1. Marc bought some bags of limes. There were 5 limes in each bag. He bought 15 limes altogether. How many bags did he buy?

_____

2. There were 10 photographs on one wall of an art gallery. The photographs were in rows, with 5 photographs in each row. How many rows were there?

_____

The problems above can be represented by multiplication equations or by **division** equations.

Problem 1   **Multiplication**   **Division**

☐ × ⑤ = 15   15 ÷ ⑤ = ☐

number   group   total   total   group   number
of groups   size   (product)   (product)   size   of groups
(factor)   (factor)   (factor)   (factor)

Problem 2   **Multiplication**   **Division**

☐ × 5 = 10   10 ÷ 5 = ☐

number   number in   total   total   number in   number
of rows   each row   (product)   (product)   each row   of rows
(factor)   (factor)   (factor)   (factor)

Here are ways to write a division. The following all mean "15 divided by 5 equals 3."

$15 ÷ 5 = 3$ $15 / 5 = 3$ $\dfrac{15}{5} = 3$

$$\begin{array}{r} 3 \leftarrow \text{quotient} \\ 5\overline{)15} \leftarrow \text{dividend} \end{array}$$

↑
divisor

The number you divide into is called the **dividend**. The number you divide by is called the **divisor**. The number that is the answer to a division problem is called the **quotient**.

► Math Tools: Equal Shares Drawings

You can use Equal Shares Drawings to help solve division problems. Here is how you might solve problem 1 on Student Activity Book page 217.

Start with the total, 15.

$15 \div ⑤ = \square$

Draw groups of 5, and connect them to the total. Count by 5s as you draw the groups. Stop when you reach 15, the total. Count how many groups you have: 3 groups.

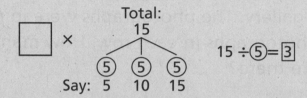

$15 \div ⑤ = \boxed{3}$

You can use a similar type of drawing to find the number of rows or columns in an array. Here is how you might solve problem 2.

Start with the total, 10.

$10 \div ⑤ = \square$

Draw rows of 5, and connect them to the total. Count by 5s as you draw the rows. Stop when you reach 10, the total. Count how many rows you have: 2 rows.

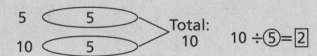

$10 \div ⑤ = \boxed{2}$

Solve each problem.

3. At a bake sale, Luisa bought a lemon square for 35¢. If she paid using only nickels, how many nickels did she spend? _____

4. Mr. Su bought a sheet of 20 stamps. There were 5 stamps in each row. How many columns of stamps were there? _____

The Meaning of Division

► **Check Sheet 1: 5s and 2s**

5s Multiplications	5s Divisions	2s Multiplications	2s Divisions
2 × 5 = 10	30 / 5 = 6	4 × 2 = 8	8 / 2 = 4
5 • 6 = 30	5 ÷ 5 = 1	2 • 8 = 16	18 ÷ 2 = 9
5 * 9 = 45	15 / 5 = 3	1 * 2 = 2	2 / 2 = 1
4 × 5 = 20	50 ÷ 5 = 10	6 × 2 = 12	16 ÷ 2 = 8
5 • 7 = 35	20 / 5 = 4	2 • 9 = 18	4 / 2 = 2
10 * 5 = 50	10 ÷ 5 = 2	2 * 2 = 4	20 ÷ 2 = 10
1 × 5 = 5	35 / 5 = 7	3 × 2 = 6	10 / 2 = 5
5 • 3 = 15	40 ÷ 5 = 8	2 • 5 = 10	12 ÷ 2 = 6
8 * 5 = 40	25 / 5 = 5	10 * 2 = 20	6 / 2 = 3
5 × 5 = 25	45 / 5 = 9	2 × 7 = 14	14 / 2 = 7
5 • 8 = 40	20 ÷ 5 = 4	2 • 10 = 20	4 ÷ 2 = 2
7 * 5 = 35	15 / 5 = 3	9 * 2 = 18	2 / 2 = 1
5 × 4 = 20	30 ÷ 5 = 6	2 × 6 = 12	8 ÷ 2 = 4
6 • 5 = 30	25 / 5 = 5	8 • 2 = 16	6 / 2 = 3
5 * 1 = 5	10 ÷ 5 = 2	2 * 3 = 6	20 ÷ 2 = 10
5 × 10 = 50	45 / 5 = 9	2 × 2 = 4	14 / 2 = 7
9 • 5 = 45	35 ÷ 5 = 7	1 • 2 = 2	10 ÷ 2 = 5
5 * 2 = 10	50 ÷ 5 = 10	2 * 4 = 8	16 ÷ 2 = 8
3 × 5 = 15	40 / 5 = 8	5 × 2 = 10	12 / 2 = 6
5 • 5 = 25	5 ÷ 5 = 1	7 • 2 = 14	18 ÷ 2 = 9

Check Sheet 1: 5s and 2s

Name _____   Date _____

▶ Check Sheet 2: 10s and 9s

10s Multiplications	10s Divisions	9s Multiplications	9s Divisions
$9 \times 10 = 90$	$100 / 10 = 10$	$3 \times 9 = 27$	$27 / 9 = 3$
$10 \cdot 3 = 30$	$50 \div 10 = 5$	$9 \cdot 7 = 63$	$9 \div 9 = 1$
$10 * 6 = 60$	$70 / 10 = 7$	$10 * 9 = 90$	$81 / 9 = 9$
$1 \times 10 = 10$	$40 \div 10 = 4$	$5 \times 9 = 45$	$45 \div 9 = 5$
$10 \cdot 4 = 40$	$80 / 10 = 8$	$9 \cdot 8 = 72$	$90 / 9 = 10$
$10 * 7 = 70$	$60 \div 10 = 6$	$9 * 1 = 9$	$36 \div 9 = 4$
$8 \times 10 = 80$	$10 / 10 = 1$	$2 \times 9 = 18$	$18 / 9 = 2$
$10 \cdot 10 = 100$	$20 \div 10 = 2$	$9 \cdot 9 = 81$	$63 \div 9 = 7$
$5 * 10 = 50$	$90 / 10 = 9$	$6 * 9 = 54$	$54 / 9 = 6$
$10 \times 2 = 20$	$30 / 10 = 3$	$9 \times 4 = 36$	$72 / 9 = 8$
$10 \cdot 5 = 50$	$80 \div 10 = 8$	$9 \cdot 5 = 45$	$27 \div 9 = 3$
$4 * 10 = 40$	$70 / 10 = 7$	$4 * 9 = 36$	$45 / 9 = 5$
$10 \times 1 = 10$	$100 \div 10 = 10$	$9 \times 1 = 9$	$63 \div 9 = 7$
$3 \cdot 10 = 30$	$90 / 10 = 9$	$3 \cdot 9 = 27$	$72 / 9 = 8$
$10 * 8 = 80$	$60 \div 10 = 6$	$9 * 8 = 72$	$54 \div 9 = 6$
$7 \times 10 = 70$	$30 / 10 = 3$	$7 \times 9 = 63$	$18 / 9 = 2$
$6 \cdot 10 = 60$	$10 \div 10 = 1$	$6 \cdot 9 = 54$	$90 \div 9 = 10$
$10 * 9 = 90$	$40 \div 10 = 4$	$9 * 9 = 81$	$9 \div 9 = 1$
$10 \times 10 = 100$	$20 / 10 = 2$	$10 \times 9 = 90$	$36 / 9 = 4$
$2 \cdot 10 = 20$	$50 \div 10 = 5$	$2 \cdot 9 = 18$	$81 \div 9 = 9$

Check Sheet 2: 10s and 9s

▶ Explore Patterns with 9s

What patterns do you see below?

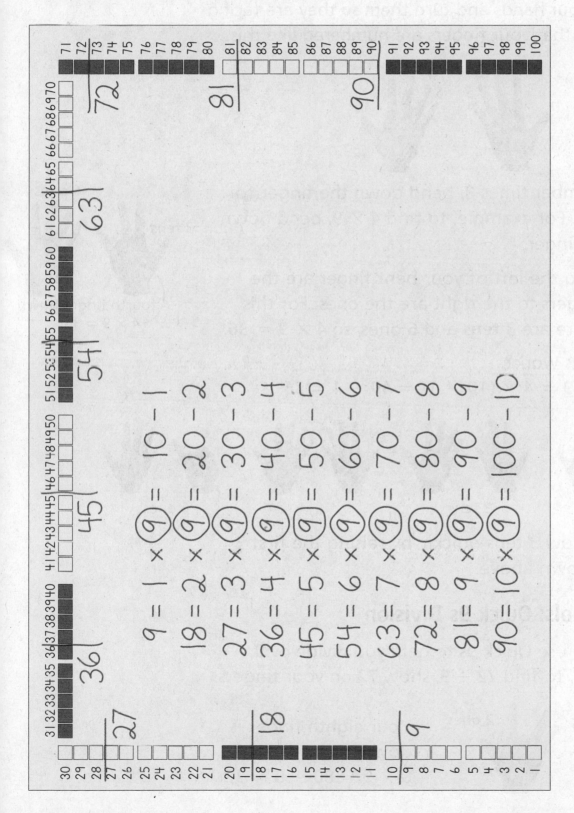

► Math Tools: Quick 9s Multiplication

You can use the Quick 9s method to help you multiply by 9. Open your hands and turn them so they are facing you. Imagine that your fingers are numbered like this.

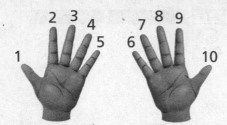

To find a number times 9, bend down the finger for that number. For example, to find 4 × 9, bend down your fourth finger.

The fingers to the left of your bent finger are the tens. The fingers to the right are the ones. For this problem, there are 3 tens and 6 ones, so 4 × 9 = 36.

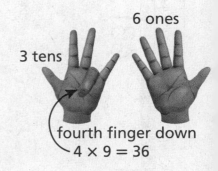

6 ones

3 tens

fourth finger down
4 × 9 = 36

Why does this work?
Because 4 × 9 = 4 × (10 − 1) = 40 − 4 = 36

3 tens   +   6 ones

You could show 3 tens quickly by raising the first 3 fingers as shown above.

► Math Tools: Quick 9s Division

You can also use Quick 9s to help you divide by 9.
For example, to find 72 ÷ 9, show 72 on your fingers.

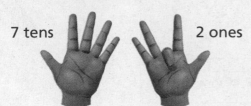

7 tens   2 ones

Your eighth finger is down, so 72 ÷ 9 = 8.
8 × 9 = 80 − 8 = 72

Class Activity

► **Sprints for 2s**

As your teacher reads each multiplication or division,
write your answer in the space provided.

× 2	÷ 2
a. _____	a. _____
b. _____	b. _____
c. _____	c. _____
d. _____	d. _____
e. _____	e. _____
f. _____	f. _____
g. _____	g. _____
h. _____	h. _____
i. _____	i. _____
j. _____	j. _____

► Check Sheet 3: 2s, 5s, 9s, and 10s

2s, 5s, 9s, 10s Multiplications	2s, 5s, 9s, 10s Multiplications	2s, 5s, 9s, 10s Divisions	2s, 5s, 9s, 10s Divisions
$2 \times 10 = 20$	$5 \times 10 = 50$	$18 / 2 = 9$	$36 / 9 = 4$
$10 \cdot 5 = 50$	$10 \cdot 9 = 90$	$50 \div 5 = 10$	$70 \div 10 = 7$
$9 * 6 = 54$	$4 * 10 = 40$	$72 / 9 = 8$	$18 / 2 = 9$
$7 \times 10 = 70$	$2 \times 9 = 18$	$60 \div 10 = 6$	$45 \div 5 = 9$
$2 \cdot 3 = 6$	$5 \cdot 3 = 15$	$12 / 2 = 6$	$45 / 9 = 5$
$5 * 7 = 35$	$6 * 9 = 54$	$30 \div 5 = 6$	$30 \div 10 = 3$
$9 \times 10 = 90$	$10 \times 3 = 30$	$18 / 9 = 2$	$6 / 2 = 3$
$6 \cdot 10 = 60$	$3 \cdot 2 = 6$	$50 \div 10 = 5$	$50 \div 5 = 10$
$8 * 2 = 16$	$5 * 8 = 40$	$14 / 2 = 7$	$27 / 9 = 3$
$5 \times 6 = 30$	$9 \times 9 = 81$	$25 / 5 = 5$	$70 / 10 = 7$
$9 \cdot 5 = 45$	$10 \cdot 4 = 40$	$81 \div 9 = 9$	$20 \div 2 = 10$
$8 * 10 = 80$	$9 * 2 = 18$	$20 / 10 = 2$	$45 / 5 = 9$
$2 \times 1 = 2$	$5 \times 1 = 5$	$8 \div 2 = 4$	$54 \div 9 = 6$
$3 \cdot 5 = 15$	$9 \cdot 6 = 54$	$45 / 5 = 9$	$80 / 10 = 8$
$4 * 9 = 36$	$10 * 1 = 10$	$63 \div 9 = 7$	$16 \div 2 = 8$
$3 \times 10 = 30$	$7 \times 2 = 14$	$30 / 10 = 3$	$15 / 5 = 3$
$2 \cdot 6 = 12$	$6 \cdot 5 = 30$	$10 \div 2 = 5$	$90 \div 9 = 10$
$4 * 5 = 20$	$8 * 9 = 72$	$40 \div 5 = 8$	$100 \div 10 = 10$
$9 \times 7 = 63$	$10 \times 6 = 60$	$9 / 9 = 1$	$12 / 2 = 6$
$1 \cdot 10 = 10$	$2 \cdot 8 = 16$	$50 \div 10 = 5$	$35 \div 5 = 7$

Study Sheet B

4s

Count-bys	Mixed Up ×	Mixed Up ÷
$1 \times 4 = 4$	$4 \times 4 = 16$	$12 \div 4 = 3$
$2 \times 4 = 8$	$1 \times 4 = 4$	$36 \div 4 = 9$
$3 \times 4 = 12$	$7 \times 4 = 28$	$24 \div 4 = 6$
$4 \times 4 = 16$	$3 \times 4 = 12$	$4 \div 4 = 1$
$5 \times 4 = 20$	$9 \times 4 = 36$	$20 \div 4 = 5$
$6 \times 4 = 24$	$10 \times 4 = 40$	$28 \div 4 = 7$
$7 \times 4 = 28$	$2 \times 4 = 8$	$8 \div 4 = 2$
$8 \times 4 = 32$	$5 \times 4 = 20$	$40 \div 4 = 10$
$9 \times 4 = 36$	$8 \times 4 = 32$	$32 \div 4 = 8$
$10 \times 4 = 40$	$6 \times 4 = 24$	$16 \div 4 = 4$

1s

Count-bys	Mixed Up ×	Mixed Up ÷
$1 \times 1 = 1$	$5 \times 1 = 5$	$10 \div 1 = 10$
$2 \times 1 = 2$	$7 \times 1 = 7$	$8 \div 1 = 8$
$3 \times 1 = 3$	$10 \times 1 = 10$	$4 \div 1 = 4$
$4 \times 1 = 4$	$1 \times 1 = 1$	$9 \div 1 = 9$
$5 \times 1 = 5$	$8 \times 1 = 8$	$6 \div 1 = 6$
$6 \times 1 = 6$	$4 \times 1 = 4$	$7 \div 1 = 7$
$7 \times 1 = 7$	$9 \times 1 = 9$	$1 \div 1 = 1$
$8 \times 1 = 8$	$3 \times 1 = 3$	$2 \div 1 = 2$
$9 \times 1 = 9$	$2 \times 1 = 2$	$5 \div 1 = 5$
$10 \times 1 = 10$	$6 \times 1 = 6$	$3 \div 1 = 3$

3s

Count-bys	Mixed Up ×	Mixed Up ÷
$1 \times 3 = 3$	$5 \times 3 = 15$	$27 \div 3 = 9$
$2 \times 3 = 6$	$1 \times 3 = 3$	$6 \div 3 = 2$
$3 \times 3 = 9$	$8 \times 3 = 24$	$18 \div 3 = 6$
$4 \times 3 = 12$	$10 \times 3 = 30$	$30 \div 3 = 10$
$5 \times 3 = 15$	$3 \times 3 = 9$	$9 \div 3 = 3$
$6 \times 3 = 18$	$7 \times 3 = 21$	$3 \div 3 = 1$
$7 \times 3 = 21$	$9 \times 3 = 27$	$12 \div 3 = 4$
$8 \times 3 = 24$	$2 \times 3 = 6$	$24 \div 3 = 8$
$9 \times 3 = 27$	$4 \times 3 = 12$	$15 \div 3 = 5$
$10 \times 3 = 30$	$6 \times 3 = 18$	$21 \div 3 = 7$

0s

Count-bys	Mixed Up ×
$1 \times 0 = 0$	$3 \times 0 = 0$
$2 \times 0 = 0$	$10 \times 0 = 0$
$3 \times 0 = 0$	$5 \times 0 = 0$
$4 \times 0 = 0$	$8 \times 0 = 0$
$5 \times 0 = 0$	$7 \times 0 = 0$
$6 \times 0 = 0$	$2 \times 0 = 0$
$7 \times 0 = 0$	$9 \times 0 = 0$
$8 \times 0 = 0$	$6 \times 0 = 0$
$9 \times 0 = 0$	$1 \times 0 = 0$
$10 \times 0 = 0$	$4 \times 0 = 0$

Study Sheet B

2×2

$\begin{array}{r} 2 \\ \times 3 \end{array}$ $\begin{array}{r} 3 \\ \times 2 \end{array}$

2×4
4×2

$\begin{array}{r} 2 \\ \times 5 \end{array}$ $\begin{array}{r} 5 \\ \times 2 \end{array}$

2×6
6×2

$\begin{array}{r} 2 \\ \times 7 \end{array}$ $\begin{array}{r} 7 \\ \times 2 \end{array}$

2×8
8×2

$\begin{array}{r} 2 \\ \times 9 \end{array}$ $\begin{array}{r} 9 \\ \times 2 \end{array}$

Multiplication Strategy Cards

Card 1:

$10 = 2 \times 5$

$10 = 5 \times 2$

```
5    2
10   4
     6
     8
     10
```

```
   5
2 [· · · · ·]
  [·  10   ]
```

Card 2:

$$\begin{array}{c} 2 \\ \times 4 \\ \hline 8 \end{array} \qquad \begin{array}{c} 4 \\ \times 2 \\ \hline 8 \end{array}$$

```
2    4
4    8
6
8
```

```
  2
4 [·]
  [· 8]
  [·]
  [·]
```

Card 3:

$6 = 2 \times 3$

$6 = 3 \times 2$

```
3    2
6    4
     6
```

```
   3
2 [· · ·]
  [· 6 ]
```

Card 4:

$$\begin{array}{c} 2 \\ \times 2 \\ \hline 4 \end{array}$$

```
2
4
```

```
  2
2 [· ·]
  [4 ]
```

Card 5:

$18 = 2 \times 9$

$18 = 9 \times 2$

```
9     2
18    4
      6
      8
      10
      12
      14
      16
      18
```

```
      9
2 [· · · · · · · · ·]
  [·       18      ]
```

Card 6:

$$\begin{array}{c} 2 \\ \times 8 \\ \hline 16 \end{array} \qquad \begin{array}{c} 8 \\ \times 2 \\ \hline 16 \end{array}$$

```
8     2
16    4
      6
      8
      10
      12
      14
      16
```

```
  2
  [·]
  [·]
  [·]
  [·]
8 [· 16]
  [·]
  [·]
  [·]
  [·]
```

Card 7:

$14 = 2 \times 7$

$14 = 7 \times 2$

```
7     2
14    4
      6
      8
      10
      12
      14
```

```
      7
2 [· · · · · · ·]
  [·    14     ]
```

Card 8:

$$\begin{array}{c} 2 \\ \times 6 \\ \hline 12 \end{array} \qquad \begin{array}{c} 6 \\ \times 2 \\ \hline 12 \end{array}$$

```
6     2
12    4
      6
      8
      10
      12
```

```
  2
  [·]
  [·]
6 [· 12]
  [·]
  [·]
  [·]
```

Multiplication Strategy Cards

3×3

$$\begin{array}{r} 3 \\ \times\ 4 \\ \hline \end{array} \qquad \begin{array}{r} 4 \\ \times\ 3 \\ \hline \end{array}$$

3×5
5×3

$$\begin{array}{r} 3 \\ \times\ 6 \\ \hline \end{array} \qquad \begin{array}{r} 6 \\ \times\ 3 \\ \hline \end{array}$$

3×7
7×3

$$\begin{array}{r} 3 \\ \times\ 8 \\ \hline \end{array} \qquad \begin{array}{r} 8 \\ \times\ 3 \\ \hline \end{array}$$

3×9
9×3

$$\begin{array}{r} 4 \\ \times\ 4 \\ \hline \end{array}$$

Card 1
$$18 = 3 \times 6$$
$$18 = 6 \times 3$$

6	3
12	6
18	9
	12
	15
	18

6
3 ∘ 18

Card 2
$$\begin{array}{r} 3 \\ \times 5 \\ \hline 15 \end{array} \qquad \begin{array}{r} 5 \\ \times 3 \\ \hline 15 \end{array}$$

5	3
10	6
15	9
	12
	15

3
5 ∘ 15

Card 3
$$12 = 3 \times 4$$
$$12 = 4 \times 3$$

4	3
8	6
12	9
	12

4
3 ∘ 12

Card 4
$$\begin{array}{r} 3 \\ \times 3 \\ \hline 9 \end{array}$$

3
6
9

3
3 ∘ 9

Card 5
$$16 = 4 \times 4$$

4
8
12
16

4
4 ∘ 16

Card 6
$$\begin{array}{r} 3 \\ \times 9 \\ \hline 27 \end{array} \qquad \begin{array}{r} 9 \\ \times 3 \\ \hline 27 \end{array}$$

9	3
18	6
27	9
	12
	15
	18
	21
	24
	27

9
3 ∘ 27

Card 7
$$24 = 3 \times 8$$
$$24 = 8 \times 3$$

8	3
16	6
24	9
	12
	15
	18
	21
	24

3
8 ∘ 24

Card 8
$$\begin{array}{r} 3 \\ \times 7 \\ \hline 21 \end{array} \qquad \begin{array}{r} 7 \\ \times 3 \\ \hline 21 \end{array}$$

7	3
14	6
21	9
	12
	15
	18
	21

7
3 ∘ 21

Multiplication Strategy Cards

4×5
5×4

$$\begin{array}{r} 4 \\ \times 6 \end{array} \qquad \begin{array}{r} 6 \\ \times 4 \end{array}$$

4×7
7×4

$$\begin{array}{r} 4 \\ \times 8 \end{array} \qquad \begin{array}{r} 8 \\ \times 4 \end{array}$$

4×9
9×4

$$\begin{array}{r} 5 \\ \times 5 \end{array}$$

5×6
6×5

$$\begin{array}{r} 5 \\ \times 7 \end{array} \qquad \begin{array}{r} 7 \\ \times 5 \end{array}$$

$32 = 4 \times 8$	
$32 = 8 \times 4$	

8   4
16   8
24   12
32   16
    20
    24
    28
    32

4
8   32

$4 \quad\quad 7$
$\times 7 \quad \times 4$
$28 \quad\quad 28$

7   4
14   8
21   12
28   16
    20
    24
    28

7
4   28

$24 = 4 \times 6$
$24 = 6 \times 4$

6   4
12   8
18   12
24   16
    20
    24

4
6   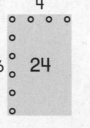 24

$4 \quad\quad 5$
$\times 5 \quad \times 4$
$20 \quad\quad 20$

5   4
10   8
15   12
20   16
    20

5
4   20

$35 = 5 \times 7$
$35 = 7 \times 5$

7   5
14   10
21   15
28   20
35   25
    30
    35

7
5   35

$5 \quad\quad 6$
$\times 6 \quad \times 5$
$30 \quad\quad 30$

6   5
12   10
18   15
24   20
30   25
    30

5
6   30

$25 = 5 \times 5$

5
10
15
20
25

5
5   25

$4 \quad\quad 9$
$\times 9 \quad \times 4$
$36 \quad\quad 36$

9   4
18   8
27   12
36   16
    20
    24
    28
    32
    36

9
4   36

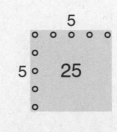

Multiplication Strategy Cards

5×8 8×5	$\begin{matrix}5\\ \times 9\end{matrix}$ $\begin{matrix}9\\ \times 5\end{matrix}$	6×6	$\begin{matrix}6\\ \times 7\end{matrix}$ $\begin{matrix}7\\ \times 6\end{matrix}$
6×8 8×6	$\begin{matrix}6\\ \times 9\end{matrix}$ $\begin{matrix}9\\ \times 6\end{matrix}$	7×7	$\begin{matrix}7\\ \times 8\end{matrix}$ $\begin{matrix}8\\ \times 7\end{matrix}$

Card 1

$42 = 7 \times 6$

$42 = 6 \times 7$

6	7
12	14
18	21
24	28
30	35
36	42
42	

7

6 | 42

Card 2

$\times \frac{6}{36}$ 6

6
12
18
24
30

36

6

6 | 36

Card 3

$45 = 9 \times 5$

$45 = 5 \times 9$

5	9
10	18
15	27
20	36
25	45
30	
35	
40	
45	

9

5 | 45

Card 4

$\times \frac{5}{40}$ 8 $\times \frac{8}{40}$ 5

5	8
10	16
15	24
20	32
25	40
30	
35	
40	

5

8 | 40

Card 5

$56 = 7 \times 8$

$56 = 8 \times 7$

8	7
16	14
24	21
32	28
40	35
48	42
56	49
	56

8

7 | 56

Card 6

$\times \frac{7}{49}$ 7

7
14
21
28
35

42
49

7

7 | 49

Card 7

$54 = 9 \times 6$

$54 = 6 \times 9$

6	9
12	18
18	27
24	36
30	45
36	54
42	
48	
54	

9

6 | 54

Card 8

$\times \frac{8}{48}$ 6 $\times \frac{6}{48}$ 8

6	8
12	16
18	24
24	32
30	40
36	48
42	
48	

8

6 | 48

Multiplication Strategy Cards

7×9
9×7

8
$\times 8$

9×8
8×9

9
$\times 9$

Card 1: 81 = 9 × 9

9
18
27
36
45

54
63
72
81

9
9 | 81

Card 2:

$$9 \times 8 = 72 \qquad 8 \times 9 = 72$$

8
16
24
32
40

48
56
64
72

9
18
27
36
45

54
63
72

9
8 | 72

Card 3: 64 = 8 × 8

8
16
24
32
40

48
56
64

8
8 | 64

Card 4:

$$7 \times 9 = 63 \qquad 9 \times 7 = 63$$

9
18
27
36
45

54
63

7
14
21
28
35

42
49
56
63

9
7 | 63

Multiplication Strategy Cards

$2\overline{)4}$

$4 \div 2$

$2\overline{)6}$

$6 \div 2$

$2\overline{)8}$

$8 \div 2$

$2\overline{)10}$

$10 \div 2$

$2\overline{)12}$

$12 \div 2$

$2\overline{)14}$

$14 \div 2$

$2\overline{)16}$

$16 \div 2$

$2\overline{)18}$

$18 \div 2$

Row 1

Card 1:

5
$2\overline{)10}$ $5\overline{)10}$

2   5
4   10
6
8
10

5
$2\;\underset{\circ}{\circ\circ\;\circ\circ\circ}$
    10

Card 2:

4
$2\overline{)8}$ $4\overline{)8}$

2   4
4   8
6
8

4
$2\;\underset{\circ}{\circ\circ\;\circ\circ}$
    8

Card 3:

3
$2\overline{)6}$ $3\overline{)6}$

2   3
4   6
6

3
$2\;\underset{\circ}{\circ\circ\;\circ}$
    6

Card 4:

2
$2\overline{)4}$

2
4

2
$2\;\underset{\circ}{\circ\circ}$
    4

Row 2

Card 5:

9
$2\overline{)18}$ $9\overline{)18}$

2   9
4   18
6
8
10

12
14
16
18

9
$2\;\underset{\circ}{\circ\circ\;\circ\circ\circ\circ\circ\circ\circ}$
    18

Card 6:

8
$2\overline{)16}$ $8\overline{)16}$

2   8
4   16
6
8
10

12
14
16

8
$2\;\underset{\circ}{\circ\circ\;\circ\circ\circ\circ\circ\circ}$
    16

Card 7:

7
$2\overline{)14}$ $7\overline{)14}$

2   7
4   14
6
8
10

12
14

7
$2\;\underset{\circ}{\circ\circ\;\circ\circ\circ\circ\circ}$
    14

Card 8:

6
$2\overline{)12}$ $6\overline{)12}$

2   6
4   12
6
8
10

12

6
$2\;\underset{\circ}{\circ\circ\;\circ\circ\circ\circ}$
    12

Division Strategy Cards

$3\overline{)6}$

$6 \div 3$

$4\overline{)8}$

$8 \div 4$

$5\overline{)10}$

$10 \div 5$

$6\overline{)12}$

$12 \div 6$

$7\overline{)14}$

$14 \div 7$

$8\overline{)16}$

$16 \div 8$

$9\overline{)18}$

$18 \div 9$

$3\overline{)9}$

$9 \div 3$

Division problem cards:

Card 1:
$$6\overline{)12} \quad 2\overline{)12}$$
with quotients 2 and 6
6, 12 | 2, 4, 6, 8, 10, 12

Card 2:
$$5\overline{)10} \quad 2\overline{)10}$$
with quotients 2 and 5
5, 10 | 2, 4, 6, 8, 10

Card 3:
$$4\overline{)8} \quad 2\overline{)8}$$
with quotients 2 and 4
4, 8 | 2, 4, 6, 8

Card 4:
$$3\overline{)6} \quad 2\overline{)6}$$
with quotients 2 and 3
3, 6 | 2, 4, 6

Card 5:
$$3\overline{)9}$$
with quotient 3
3, 6, 9

Card 6:
$$9\overline{)18} \quad 2\overline{)18}$$
with quotients 2 and 9
9, 18 | 2, 4, 6, 8, 10, 12, 14, 16, 18

Card 7:
$$8\overline{)16} \quad 2\overline{)16}$$
with quotients 2 and 8
8, 16 | 2, 4, 6, 8, 10, 12, 14, 16

Card 8:
$$7\overline{)14} \quad 2\overline{)14}$$
with quotients 2 and 7
7, 14 | 2, 4, 6, 8, 10, 12, 14

Division Strategy Cards

$3 \overline{)12}$	$3 \overline{)15}$	$3 \overline{)18}$	$3 \overline{)21}$
$12 \div 3$	$15 \div 3$	$18 \div 3$	$21 \div 3$

$3 \overline{)24}$	$3 \overline{)27}$	$4 \overline{)12}$	$5 \overline{)15}$
$24 \div 3$	$27 \div 3$	$12 \div 4$	$15 \div 5$

Division Strategy Cards

Card 1

$$7 \quad\quad 3$$
$$3\overline{)21} \quad 7\overline{)21}$$

3	7
6	14
9	21
12	
15	
18	
21	

7
3 — 21

Card 2

$$6 \quad\quad 3$$
$$3\overline{)18} \quad 6\overline{)18}$$

3	6
6	12
9	18
12	
15	
18	

6
3 — 18

Card 3

$$5 \quad\quad 3$$
$$3\overline{)15} \quad 5\overline{)15}$$

3	5
6	10
9	15
12	
15	

5
3 — 15

Card 4

$$4 \quad\quad 3$$
$$3\overline{)12} \quad 4\overline{)12}$$

3	4
6	8
9	12
12	

4
3 — 12

Card 5

$$3 \quad\quad 5$$
$$5\overline{)15} \quad 3\overline{)15}$$

5	3
10	6
15	9
	12
	15

3
5 — 15

Card 6

$$3 \quad\quad 4$$
$$4\overline{)12} \quad 3\overline{)12}$$

4	3
8	6
12	9
	12

3
4 — 12

Card 7

$$9 \quad\quad 3$$
$$3\overline{)27} \quad 9\overline{)27}$$

3	9
6	18
9	27
12	
15	
18	
21	
24	
27	

9
3 — 27

Card 8

$$8 \quad\quad 3$$
$$3\overline{)24} \quad 8\overline{)24}$$

3	8
6	16
9	24
12	
15	
18	
21	
24	

8
3 — 24

Division Strategy Cards

$6 \overline{)18}$

$18 \div 6$

$7 \overline{)21}$

$21 \div 7$

$8 \overline{)24}$

$24 \div 8$

$9 \overline{)27}$

$27 \div 9$

$4 \overline{)16}$

$16 \div 4$

$4 \overline{)20}$

$20 \div 4$

$4 \overline{)24}$

$24 \div 4$

$4 \overline{)28}$

$28 \div 4$

Division Strategy Cards

$4\overline{)32}$	$4\overline{)36}$	$5\overline{)20}$	$6\overline{)24}$
$32 \div 4$	$36 \div 4$	$20 \div 5$	$24 \div 6$

$7\overline{)28}$	$8\overline{)32}$	$9\overline{)36}$	$5\overline{)25}$
$28 \div 7$	$32 \div 8$	$36 \div 9$	$25 \div 5$

Division Strategy Cards

Row 1

Card 1:

4 / 6)24
6)24 4)24

6	4
12	8
18	12
24	16
	20
	24

4
6 • 24

Card 2:

4 / 5
5)20 4)20

5	4
10	8
15	12
20	16
	20

4
5 • 20

Card 3:

9 / 4
4)36 9)36

4	9
8	18
12	27
16	36
20	
24	
28	
32	
36	

9
4 • 36

Card 4:

8 / 4
4)32 8)32

4	8
8	16
12	24
16	32
20	
24	
28	
32	

8
4 • 32

Row 2

Card 5:

5
5)25

5
10
15
20
25

5
5 • 25

Card 6:

4 / 9
9)36 4)36

9	4
18	8
27	12
36	16
	20
	24
	28
	32
	36

4
9 • 36

Card 7:

4 / 8
8)32 4)32

8	4
16	8
24	12
32	16
	20
	24
	28
	32

4
8 • 32

Card 8:

4 / 7
7)28 4)28

7	4
14	8
21	12
28	16
	20
	24
	28

4
7 • 28

Division Strategy Cards

$5 \overline{)30}$	$5 \overline{)35}$	$5 \overline{)40}$	$5 \overline{)45}$
$30 \div 5$	$35 \div 5$	$40 \div 5$	$45 \div 5$

$6 \overline{)30}$	$7 \overline{)35}$	$8 \overline{)40}$	$9 \overline{)45}$
$30 \div 6$	$35 \div 7$	$40 \div 8$	$45 \div 9$

Row 1

Card 1: 9 | 5 — 5)45 9)45

5	9
10	18
15	27
20	36
25	45
30	
35	
40	
45	

Array: 9 across, 5 down, 45

Card 2: 8 | 5 — 5)40 8)40

5	8
10	16
15	24
20	32
25	40
30	
35	
40	

Array: 8 across, 5 down, 40

Card 3: 7 | 5 — 5)35 7)35

5	7
10	14
15	21
20	28
25	35
30	
35	

Array: 7 across, 5 down, 35

Card 4: 6 | 5 — 5)30 6)30

5	6
10	12
15	18
20	24
25	30
30	

Array: 6 across, 5 down, 30

Row 2

Card 5: 5 | 9 — 9)45 5)45

9	5
18	10
27	15
36	20
45	25
	30
	35
	40
	45

Array: 5 across, 9 down, 45

Card 6: 5 | 8 — 8)40 5)40

8	5
16	10
24	15
32	20
40	25
	30
	35
	40

Array: 5 across, 8 down, 40

Card 7: 5 | 7 — 7)35 5)35

7	5
14	10
21	15
28	20
35	25
	30
	35

Array: 5 across, 7 down, 35

Card 8: 5 | 6 — 6)30 5)30

6	5
12	10
18	15
24	20
30	25
	30

Array: 5 across, 6 down, 30

Division Strategy Cards

$6\overline{)36}$	$6\overline{)42}$	$6\overline{)48}$	$6\overline{)54}$
$36 \div 6$	$42 \div 6$	$48 \div 6$	$54 \div 6$

$7\overline{)42}$	$8\overline{)48}$	$9\overline{)54}$	$7\overline{)49}$
$42 \div 7$	$48 \div 8$	$54 \div 9$	$49 \div 7$

Division Strategy Cards

Row 1

Card 1:

$$9 \quad 6$$
$$6\overline{)54} \quad 9\overline{)54}$$

6	9
12	18
18	27
24	36
30	45
36	54
42	
48	
54	

9

6 54

Card 2:

$$8 \quad 6$$
$$6\overline{)48} \quad 8\overline{)48}$$

6	8
12	16
18	24
24	32
30	40
36	48
42	
48	

8

6 48

Card 3:

$$7 \quad 6$$
$$6\overline{)42} \quad 7\overline{)42}$$

6	7
12	14
18	21
24	28
30	35
36	42
42	

7

6 42

Card 4:

$$6$$
$$6\overline{)36}$$

6
12
18
24
30
36

6

6 36

Row 2

Card 5:

$$7$$
$$7\overline{)49}$$

7
14
21
28
35
42
49

7

7 49

Card 6:

$$6 \quad 9$$
$$9\overline{)54} \quad 6\overline{)54}$$

9	6
18	12
27	18
36	24
45	30
54	36
	42
	48
	54

6

9 54

Card 7:

$$6 \quad 8$$
$$8\overline{)48} \quad 6\overline{)48}$$

8	6
16	12
24	18
32	24
40	30
48	36
	42
	48

6

8 48

Card 8:

$$6 \quad 7$$
$$7\overline{)42} \quad 6\overline{)42}$$

7	6
14	12
21	18
28	24
35	30
42	36
	42

6

7 42

Division Strategy Cards

$7\overline{)56}$	$7\overline{)63}$	$8\overline{)56}$	$9\overline{)63}$
$56 \div 7$	$63 \div 7$	$56 \div 8$	$63 \div 9$

$8\overline{)64}$	$8\overline{)72}$	$9\overline{)72}$	$9\overline{)81}$
$64 \div 8$	$72 \div 8$	$72 \div 9$	$81 \div 9$

Division Strategy Cards

Card 1

$$7 \overline{)63} \rightarrow 9\overline{)63}$$
$$9 \rightarrow 7\overline{)63}$$

9	7
18	14
27	21
36	28
45	35
54	42
63	49
	56
	63

7

9 · 63

Card 2

$$7\overline{)56} \qquad 8\overline{)56}$$
$$8\overline{)56} \qquad 7\overline{)56}$$

8	7
16	14
24	21
32	28
40	35
48	42
56	49
	56

7

8 · 56

Card 3

$$9\overline{)63} \qquad 7\overline{)63}$$

7	9
14	18
21	27
28	36
35	45
42	54
49	63
56	
63	

9

7 · 63

Card 4

$$8\overline{)56} \qquad 7\overline{)56}$$

7	8
14	16
21	24
28	32
35	40
42	48
49	56
56	

8

7 · 56

Card 5

$$9\overline{)81}$$

9
18
27
36
45
54
63
72
81

9

9 · 81

Card 6

$$8\overline{)72} \qquad 9\overline{)72}$$

9	8
18	16
27	24
36	32
45	40
54	48
63	56
72	64
	72

8

9 · 72

Card 7

$$9\overline{)72} \qquad 8\overline{)72}$$

8	9
16	18
24	27
32	36
40	45
48	54
56	63
64	72
72	

9

8 · 72

Card 8

$$8\overline{)64}$$

8
16
24
32
40
48
56
64

8

8 · 64

Going Further

▶ Multiply Using Patterns

Use mental math and patterns to complete.

1. $3 \times 4 = $ _12_
    $3 \times 40 = $ ____

2. $10 \times 2 = $ ____
    $100 \times 2 = $ _200_

3. $9 \times 8 = $ _72_
    $9 \times 80 = $ ____

4. $2 \times 9 = $ _18_
    $2 \times 90 = $ ____
    $2 \times 900 = $ ____

5. $5 \times 5 = $ _25_
    $5 \times 50 = $ _100_
    $5 \times 500 = $ ____

6. $3 \times 4 = $ _12_
    $3 \times 40 = $ ____
    $3 \times 400 = $ ____

7. $1 \times 1 = $ ____
    $10 \times 1 = $ ____
    $100 \times 1 = $ ____

8. $2 \times 3 = $ _6_
    $20 \times 3 = $ ____
    $200 \times 30 = $ ____

9. $5 \times 6 = $ _30_
    $5 \times 60 = $ ____
    $5 \times 600 = $ ____

10. $2 \times 4 = $ ____
    $2 \times 40 = $ ____
    $2 \times 400 = $ ____

11. $5 \times 3 = $ _15_
    $5 \times 30 = $ ____
    $5 \times 300 = $ ____

12. $9 \times 2 = $ _18_
    $9 \times 20 = $ ____
    $9 \times 200 = $ ____

13. $2 \times 30 = $ ____

14. $5 \times 40 = $ ____

15. $9 \times 60 = $ ____

16. $3 \times 80 = $ ____

17. $2 \times 70 = $ ____

18. $5 \times 90 = $ ____

19. $9 \times 500 = $ ____

20. $5 \times 200 = $ ____

21. $3 \times 300 = $ ____

22. $5 \times 800 = $ ____

23. $9 \times 900 = $ ____

24. $5 \times 600 = $ ____

25. **On the Back** Describe a pattern you can use to find
    4×200.

_____

_____

_____

_____

_____

_____

_____

_____

_____

_____

_____

_____

_____

_____

_____

_____

Solve and Create Word Problems

▶Check Sheet 4: 3s and 4s

3s Multiplications	3s Divisions	4s Multiplications	4s Divisions
$8 \times 3 = 24$	$9 / 3 = 3$	$1 \times 4 = 4$	$40 / 4 = 10$
$3 \cdot 2 = 6$	$21 \div 3 = 7$	$4 \cdot 5 = 20$	$12 \div 4 = 3$
$3 * 5 = 15$	$27 / 3 = 9$	$8 * 4 = 32$	$24 / 4 = 6$
$10 \times 3 = 30$	$3 \div 3 = 1$	$3 \times 4 = 12$	$8 \div 4 = 2$
$3 \cdot 3 = 9$	$18 / 3 = 6$	$4 \cdot 6 = 24$	$4 / 4 = 1$
$3 * 6 = 18$	$12 \div 3 = 4$	$4 * 9 = 36$	$28 \div 4 = 7$
$7 \times 3 = 21$	$30 / 3 = 10$	$10 \times 4 = 40$	$32 / 4 = 8$
$3 \cdot 9 = 27$	$6 \div 3 = 2$	$4 \cdot 7 = 28$	$16 \div 4 = 4$
$4 * 3 = 12$	$24 / 3 = 8$	$4 * 4 = 16$	$36 / 4 = 9$
$3 \times 1 = 3$	$15 / 3 = 5$	$2 \times 4 = 8$	$20 / 4 = 5$
$3 \cdot 4 = 12$	$21 \div 3 = 7$	$4 \cdot 3 = 12$	$4 \div 4 = 1$
$3 * 3 = 9$	$3 / 3 = 1$	$4 * 2 = 8$	$32 / 4 = 8$
$3 \times 10 = 30$	$9 \div 3 = 3$	$9 \times 4 = 36$	$8 \div 4 = 2$
$2 \cdot 3 = 6$	$27 / 3 = 9$	$1 \cdot 4 = 4$	$16 / 4 = 4$
$3 * 7 = 21$	$30 \div 3 = 10$	$4 * 6 = 24$	$36 \div 4 = 9$
$6 \times 3 = 18$	$18 / 3 = 6$	$5 \times 4 = 20$	$12 / 4 = 3$
$5 \cdot 3 = 15$	$6 \div 3 = 2$	$4 \cdot 4 = 16$	$40 \div 4 = 10$
$3 * 8 = 24$	$15 \div 3 = 5$	$7 * 4 = 28$	$20 \div 4 = 5$
$9 \times 3 = 27$	$12 / 3 = 4$	$8 \times 4 = 32$	$24 / 4 = 6$
$2 \cdot 3 = 6$	$24 \div 3 = 8$	$10 \cdot 4 = 40$	$28 \div 4 = 7$

▶Use Multiplications You Know

You can combine multiplications to find other multiplications.

This Equal-Shares Drawing shows that 7 groups of 4 is the same as 5 groups of 4 plus 2 groups of 4.

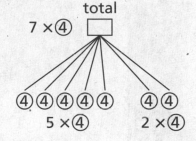

5. Find 5 ×④ and 2 ×④ and add the answers.

   _____

6. Find 7 ×④. Did you get the same answer as in exercise 5?

   _____

7. Find this product: 5 × 4 = _20_

8. Find this product: 4 × 4 = _16_

9. Use your answers to exercises 7 and 8 to find this product: 9 × 4 = _____.

▶The Puzzled Penguin

Dear Math Students:

Today I had to find 8 × 4. I didn't know the answer, but I figured it out by combining two multiplications I did know:

$$5 \times 2 = 10$$
$$3 \times 2 = 6$$
$$\overline{8 \times 4 = 16}$$

Is my answer right? If not, please help me understand why it is wrong.

Thank you,
The Puzzled Penguin

10. **On the Back** Make a drawing to show that your answers to exercises 7–9 are correct.

Name _____ Date _____

Multiply and Divide with 4

▶ Sprints for 3s

As your teacher reads each multiplication or division, write your answer in the space provided.

× 3	÷ 3
a. _____	a. _____
b. _____	b. _____
c. _____	c. _____
d. _____	d. _____
e. _____	e. _____
f. _____	f. _____
g. _____	g. _____
h. _____	h. _____
i. _____	i. _____
j. _____	j. _____

Use the Strategy Cards

►Play *Solve the Stack*

Read the rules for playing *Solve the Stack*. Then play the game with your group.

Rules for *Solve the Stack*

Number of players: 2–4
What you will need: 1 set of multiplication and division Strategy Cards

1. Shuffle the cards. Place them exercise side up in the center of the table.

2. Players take turns. On each turn, a player finds the answer to the multiplication or division on the top card and then turns the card over to check the answer.

3. If a player's answer is correct, he or she takes the card. If it is incorrect, the card is placed at the bottom of the stack.

4. Play ends when there are no more cards in the stack. The player with the most cards wins.

Class Activity

▶Explore Patterns with 1s

What patterns do you see below?

1.

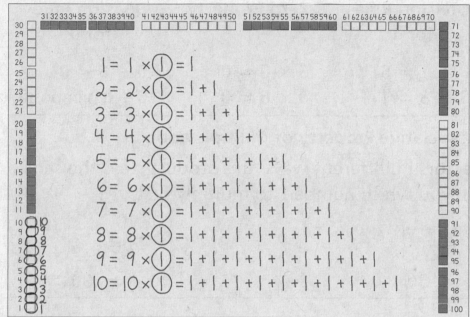

$1 = 1 \times \textcircled{1} = 1$

$2 = 2 \times \textcircled{1} = 1 + 1$

$3 = 3 \times \textcircled{1} = 1 + 1 + 1$

$4 = 4 \times \textcircled{1} = 1 + 1 + 1 + 1$

$5 = 5 \times \textcircled{1} = 1 + 1 + 1 + 1 + 1$

$6 = 6 \times \textcircled{1} = 1 + 1 + 1 + 1 + 1 + 1$

$7 = 7 \times \textcircled{1} = 1 + 1 + 1 + 1 + 1 + 1 + 1$

$8 = 8 \times \textcircled{1} = 1 + 1 + 1 + 1 + 1 + 1 + 1 + 1$

$9 = 9 \times \textcircled{1} = 1 + 1 + 1 + 1 + 1 + 1 + 1 + 1 + 1$

$10 = 10 \times \textcircled{1} = 1 + 1 + 1 + 1 + 1 + 1 + 1 + 1 + 1 + 1$

▶Explore Patterns with 0s

What patterns do you see below?

2.

$1 \times \textcircled{0} = 0$

$2 \times \textcircled{0} = 0 + 0$

$3 \times \textcircled{0} = 0 + 0 + 0$

$4 \times \textcircled{0} = 0 + 0 + 0 + 0$

$5 \times \textcircled{0} = 0 + 0 + 0 + 0 + 0$

$6 \times \textcircled{0} = 0 + 0 + 0 + 0 + 0 + 0$

$7 \times \textcircled{0} = 0 + 0 + 0 + 0 + 0 + 0 + 0$

$8 \times \textcircled{0} = 0 + 0 + 0 + 0 + 0 + 0 + 0 + 0$

$9 \times \textcircled{0} = 0 + 0 + 0 + 0 + 0 + 0 + 0 + 0 + 0$

$10 \times \textcircled{0} = 0 + 0 + 0 + 0 + 0 + 0 + 0 + 0 + 0 + 0$

► Multiplication Properties and Division Rules

Properties and Rules

Property for 1	Division Rule for 1	Zero Property	Division Rule for 0
$1 \times 6 = 6$ $6 \times 1 = 6$	$8 \div 1 = 8$ $8 \div 8 = 1$	$6 \times 0 = 0$ $0 \times 6 = 0$	$0 \div 6 = 0$ $6 \div 0$ is impossible.

Associative Property of Multiplication

When you group factors in different ways, the product stays the same. The parentheses tell you which numbers to multiply first.

$$(3 \times 2) \times 5 = \boxed{}$$
$$6 \quad \times 5 = 30$$

$$3 \times (2 \times 5) = \boxed{}$$
$$3 \times \quad 10 \quad = 30$$

Find each product.

3. $2 \times (6 \times 1) = \boxed{12}$ **4.** $(4 \times 2) \times 2 = \boxed{16}$ **5.** $7 \times (1 \times 5) = \boxed{35}$

6. $(9 \times 8) \times 0 = \boxed{72}$ **7.** $3 \times (2 \times 3) = \boxed{18}$ **8.** $6 \times (0 \times 7) = \boxed{0}$

Solve each problem.

Show your work.

9. Shawn gave 1 nickel to each of his sisters. If he gave away 3 nickels, how many sisters does Shawn have? _____

10. Kara has 3 boxes. She put 0 toys in each box. How many toys are in the boxes? _____

11. There are 3 tables in the library. Each table has 2 piles of books on it. If there are 3 books in each pile, how many books are on the tables?
_____

Multiply and Divide with 1 and 0

► **Sprints for 4s**

As your teacher reads each multiplication or division, write your answer in the space provided.

× 4	÷ 4
a. _____	a. _____
b. _____	b. _____
c. _____	c. _____
d. _____	d. _____
e. _____	e. _____
f. _____	f. _____
g. _____	g. _____
h. _____	h. _____
i. _____	i. _____
j. _____	j. _____

Play Multiplication and Division Games

▶Check Sheet 5: 1s and 0s

1s Multiplications	1s Divisions	0s Multiplications
$1 \times 4 = 4$	$10 / 1 = 10$	$4 \times 0 = 0$
$5 \cdot 1 = 5$	$5 \div 1 = 5$	$2 \cdot 0 = 0$
$7 * 1 = 7$	$7 / 1 = 7$	$0 * 8 = 0$
$1 \times 8 = 8$	$9 \div 1 = 9$	$0 \times 5 = 0$
$1 \cdot 6 = 6$	$3 / 1 = 3$	$6 \cdot 0 = 0$
$10 * 1 = 10$	$10 \div 1 = 10$	$0 * 7 = 0$
$1 \times 9 = 9$	$2 / 1 = 2$	$0 \times 2 = 0$
$3 \cdot 1 = 3$	$8 \div 1 = 8$	$0 \cdot 9 = 0$
$1 * 2 = 2$	$6 / 1 = 6$	$10 * 0 = 0$
$1 \times 1 = 1$	$9 / 1 = 9$	$1 \times 0 = 0$
$8 \cdot 1 = 8$	$1 \div 1 = 1$	$0 \cdot 6 = 0$
$1 * 7 = 7$	$5 / 1 = 5$	$9 * 0 = 0$
$1 \times 5 = 5$	$3 \div 1 = 3$	$0 \times 4 = 0$
$6 \cdot 1 = 6$	$4 / 1 = 4$	$3 \cdot 0 = 0$
$1 * 1 = 1$	$2 \div 1 = 2$	$0 * 3 = 0$
$1 \times 10 = 10$	$8 / 1 = 8$	$8 \times 0 = 0$
$9 \cdot 1 = 9$	$4 \div 1 = 4$	$0 \cdot 10 = 0$
$4 * 1 = 4$	$7 \div 1 = 7$	$0 * 1 = 0$
$2 \times 1 = 2$	$1 / 1 = 1$	$5 \times 0 = 0$
$1 \cdot 3 = 3$	$6 \div 1 = 6$	$7 \cdot 0 = 0$

▶ Check Sheet 6: Mixed 3s, 4s, 0s and 1s

3s, 4s, 0s, 1s Multiplications	3s, 4s, 0s, 1s Multiplications	3s, 4s, 1s Divisions	3s, 4s, 1s Divisions
$5 \times 3 = 15$	$0 \times 5 = 0$	$18 / 3 = 6$	$4 / 1 = 4$
$6 \cdot 4 = 24$	$10 \cdot 1 = 10$	$20 \div 4 = 5$	$21 \div 3 = 7$
$9 * 0 = 0$	$6 * 3 = 18$	$1 / 1 = 1$	$16 / 4 = 4$
$7 \times 1 = 7$	$2 \times 4 = 8$	$21 \div 3 = 7$	$9 \div 1 = 9$
$3 \cdot 3 = 9$	$5 \cdot 0 = 0$	$12 / 4 = 3$	$15 / 3 = 5$
$4 * 7 = 28$	$1 * 2 = 2$	$5 \div 1 = 5$	$8 \div 4 = 2$
$0 \times 10 = 0$	$10 \times 3 = 30$	$15 / 3 = 5$	$5 / 1 = 5$
$1 \cdot 6 = 6$	$5 \cdot 4 = 20$	$24 \div 4 = 6$	$30 \div 3 = 10$
$3 * 4 = 12$	$0 * 8 = 0$	$7 / 1 = 7$	$12 / 4 = 3$
$5 \times 4 = 20$	$9 \times 2 = 18$	$12 / 3 = 4$	$8 / 1 = 8$
$0 \cdot 5 = 0$	$10 \cdot 3 = 30$	$36 \div 4 = 9$	$27 \div 3 = 9$
$9 * 1 = 9$	$9 * 4 = 36$	$6 / 1 = 6$	$40 / 4 = 10$
$2 \times 3 = 6$	$1 \times 0 = 0$	$12 \div 3 = 4$	$4 \div 1 = 4$
$3 \cdot 4 = 12$	$1 \cdot 6 = 6$	$16 / 4 = 4$	$9 / 3 = 3$
$0 * 9 = 0$	$3 * 6 = 18$	$7 \div 1 = 7$	$16 \div 4 = 4$
$1 \times 5 = 5$	$7 \times 4 = 28$	$9 / 3 = 3$	$10 / 1 = 10$
$2 \cdot 3 = 6$	$6 \cdot 0 = 0$	$8 \div 4 = 2$	$9 \div 3 = 3$
$4 * 4 = 16$	$8 * 1 = 8$	$2 \div 1 = 2$	$20 \div 4 = 5$
$9 \times 0 = 0$	$3 \times 9 = 27$	$6 / 3 = 2$	$6 / 1 = 6$
$1 \cdot 1 = 1$	$1 \cdot 4 = 4$	$32 \div 4 = 8$	$24 \div 3 = 8$

►Play *Multiplication Three-in-a-Row*

Read the rules for playing *Multiplication Three-in-a-Row*.
Then play the game with a partner.

Rules for *Multiplication Three-in-a-Row*

Number of players: 2
What You Will Need: A set of multiplication Strategy
Cards, *Three-in-a-Row* Game Grids for each player
(see page 271)

1. Each player looks through the cards and writes any
   nine of the products in the squares of a Game Grid.
   A player may write the same product more than
   once.

2. Shuffle the cards and place them exercise side up in
   the center of the table.

3. Players take turns. On each turn, a player finds the
   answer to the multiplication on the top card and
   then turns the card over to check the answer.

4. If the answer is correct, the player looks to see if
   the product is on the game grid. If it is, the player
   puts an X through that grid square. If the answer
   is wrong, or if the product is not on the grid, the
   player does not mark anything. The player then
   puts the card problem side up on the bottom of
   the stack.

5. The first player to mark three squares in a row
   (horizontally, vertically, or diagonally) wins.

▶ Play *Division Race*

Read the rules for playing *Division Race*. Then play the game with a partner.

Rules for *Division Race*

Number of Players: 2
What You Will Need: a set of division Strategy Cards, the *Division Race* game board (see page 272), a different game piece for each player

1. Shuffle the cards and then place them exercise side up on the table.

2. Both players put their game pieces on "START."

3. Players take turns. On each turn, a player finds the answer to the division on the top card and then turns the card over to check the answer.

4. If the answer is correct, the player moves *forward* that number of spaces. If a player's answer is wrong, the player moves *back* a number of spaces equal to the *correct* answer. Players cannot move back beyond the "START" square. The player puts the card on the bottom of the stack.

5. If a player lands on a space with special instructions, he or she should follow those instructions.

6. The first player to reach "END" wins.

UNIT 7 LESSON 15

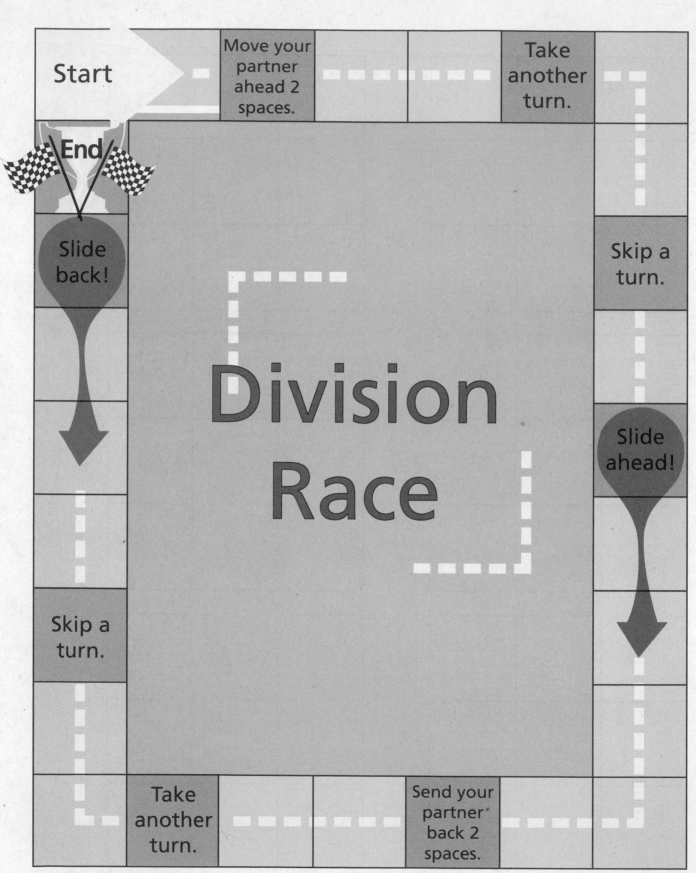

Start

End

Slide back!

Move your partner ahead 2 spaces.

Take another turn.

Skip a turn.

Slide ahead!

Division Race

Skip a turn.

Take another turn.

Send your partner back 2 spaces.

Division Race Game Board

►Check Sheet 7: 0s, 1s, 2s, 3s, 4s, 5s, 9s and 10s

0s, 1s, 2s, 3s, 4s, 5s, 9s, 10s Multiplications	0s, 1s, 2s, 3s, 4s, 5s, 9s, 10s Multiplications	1s, 2s, 3s, 4s, 5s, 9s, 10s Divisions	1s, 2s, 3s, 4s, 5s, 9s, 10s Divisions
$3 \times 0 = 0$	$0 \times 4 = 0$	$9 / 1 = 9$	$40 / 10 = 4$
$7 \cdot 1 = 7$	$5 \cdot 1 = 5$	$4 \div 2 = 2$	$7 \div 1 = 7$
$2 * 2 = 4$	$6 * 7 = 42$	$9 / 3 = 3$	$16 / 2 = 8$
$1 \times 3 = 3$	$2 \times 3 = 6$	$20 \div 4 = 5$	$18 \div 3 = 6$
$4 \cdot 4 = 16$	$5 \cdot 0 = 0$	$15 / 5 = 3$	$16 / 4 = 4$
$6 * 5 = 30$	$1 * 1 = 1$	$45 \div 9 = 5$	$50 \div 5 = 10$
$5 \times 9 = 45$	$10 \times 2 = 20$	$50 / 10 = 5$	$81 / 9 = 9$
$0 \cdot 10 = 0$	$5 \cdot 3 = 15$	$10 \div 1 = 10$	$30 \div 10 = 3$
$0 * 4 = 0$	$4 * 5 = 20$	$8 / 2 = 4$	$10 / 1 = 10$
$1 \times 8 = 8$	$5 \times 6 = 30$	$12 / 3 = 4$	$8 / 2 = 4$
$2 \cdot 5 = 10$	$9 \cdot 7 = 63$	$16 \div 4 = 4$	$27 \div 3 = 9$
$3 * 2 = 6$	$4 * 10 = 40$	$35 / 5 = 7$	$36 / 4 = 9$
$4 \times 3 = 12$	$6 \times 0 = 0$	$27 \div 9 = 3$	$30 \div 5 = 6$
$5 \cdot 4 = 20$	$1 \cdot 6 = 6$	$60 / 10 = 6$	$9 / 9 = 1$
$9 * 6 = 54$	$3 * 2 = 6$	$7 \div 1 = 7$	$80 \div 10 = 8$
$10 \times 7 = 70$	$7 \times 3 = 21$	$8 / 2 = 4$	$10 / 1 = 10$
$0 \cdot 8 = 0$	$4 \cdot 0 = 0$	$18 \div 3 = 6$	$4 \div 2 = 2$
$4 * 9 = 36$	$9 * 5 = 40$	$12 \div 4 = 3$	$21 \div 3 = 7$
$2 \times 0 = 0$	$4 \times 9 = 36$	$40 / 5 = 8$	$8 / 4 = 2$
$1 \cdot 3 = 3$	$10 \cdot 5 = 50$	$36 \div 9 = 4$	$25 \div 5 = 5$

Check Sheet 7: 0s, 1s, 2s, 3s, 4s, 5s, 9s, and 10s

▶Dashes 1–4

Complete each Dash. Check your answers on page 277.

Dash 1 2s, 5s, 9s, 10s Multiplications	Dash 2 2s, 5s, 9s, 10s Divisions	Dash 3 3s, 4s, 0s, 1s Multiplications	Dash 4 3s, 4s, 1s Divisions
a. $4 \times 5 =$ ___	a. $8 / 2 =$ ___	a. $3 \times 0 =$ ___	a. $12 / 4 =$ ___
b. $10 \cdot 3 =$ ___	b. $50 \div 10 =$ ___	b. $4 \cdot 6 =$ ___	b. $5 \div 1 =$ ___
c. $8 * 9 =$ ___	c. $15 / 5 =$ ___	c. $9 * 1 =$ ___	c. $21 / 3 =$ ___
d. $6 \times 2 =$ ___	d. $63 \div 9 =$ ___	d. $3 \times 3 =$ ___	d. $1 \div 1 =$ ___
e. $5 \cdot 7 =$ ___	e. $90 / 10 =$ ___	e. $8 \cdot 4 =$ ___	e. $16 / 4 =$ ___
f. $10 * 5 =$ ___	f. $90 \div 9 =$ ___	f. $0 * 5 =$ ___	f. $9 \div 3 =$ ___
g. $8 \times 2 =$ ___	g. $35 / 5 =$ ___	g. $1 \times 6 =$ ___	g. $32 / 4 =$ ___
h. $6 \cdot 10 =$ ___	h. $14 \div 2 =$ ___	h. $4 \cdot 3 =$ ___	h. $8 \div 1 =$ ___
i. $9 * 3 =$ ___	i. $27 / 9 =$ ___	i. $7 * 4 =$ ___	i. $24 / 4 =$ ___
j. $2 \times 9 =$ ___	j. $45 / 5 =$ ___	j. $3 \times 7 =$ ___	j. $18 / 3 =$ ___
k. $5 \cdot 8 =$ ___	k. $10 \div 10 =$ ___	k. $0 \cdot 1 =$ ___	k. $10 \div 1 =$ ___
l. $10 * 7 =$ ___	l. $25 / 5 =$ ___	l. $10 * 1 =$ ___	l. $40 / 4 =$ ___
m. $5 \times 5 =$ ___	m. $54 \div 9 =$ ___	m. $4 \times 4 =$ ___	m. $12 \div 3 =$ ___
n. $1 \cdot 5 =$ ___	n. $6 / 2 =$ ___	n. $9 \cdot 3 =$ ___	n. $6 / 3 =$ ___
o. $9 * 6 =$ ___	o. $72 \div 9 =$ ___	o. $8 * 0 =$ ___	o. $4 \div 4 =$ ___
p. $10 \times 10 =$ ___	p. $40 / 5 =$ ___	p. $5 \times 4 =$ ___	p. $7 / 1 =$ ___
q. $4 \cdot 2 =$ ___	q. $80 \div 10 =$ ___	q. $1 \cdot 6 =$ ___	q. $28 \div 4 =$ ___
r. $10 * 8 =$ ___	r. $18 \div 2 =$ ___	r. $3 * 8 =$ ___	r. $24 \div 3 =$ ___
s. $3 \times 9 =$ ___	s. $36 / 9 =$ ___	s. $4 \times 9 =$ ___	s. $20 / 4 =$ ___
t. $9 \cdot 9 =$ ___	t. $30 \div 5 =$ ___	t. $0 \cdot 4 =$ ___	t. $27 \div 3 =$ ___

▶Dashes 1–4

Complete each Dash. Check your answers on page 277.

Dash 1 2s, 5s, 9s, 10s Multiplications	Dash 2 2s, 5s, 9s, 10s Divisions	Dash 3 3s, 4s, 0s, 1s Multiplications	Dash 4 3s, 4s, 1s Divisions
a. $4 \times 5 =$ ___	a. $8 / 2 =$ ___	a. $3 \times 0 =$ ___	a. $12 / 4 =$ ___
b. $10 \cdot 3 =$ ___	b. $50 \div 10 =$ ___	b. $4 \cdot 6 =$ ___	b. $5 \div 1 =$ ___
c. $8 * 9 =$ ___	c. $15 / 5 =$ ___	c. $9 * 1 =$ ___	c. $21 / 3 =$ ___
d. $6 \times 2 =$ ___	d. $63 \div 9 =$ ___	d. $3 \times 3 =$ ___	d. $1 \div 1 =$ ___
e. $5 \cdot 7 =$ ___	e. $90 / 10 =$ ___	e. $8 \cdot 4 =$ ___	e. $16 / 4 =$ ___
f. $10 * 5 =$ ___	f. $90 \div 9 =$ ___	f. $0 * 5 =$ ___	f. $9 \div 3 =$ ___
g. $8 \times 2 =$ ___	g. $35 / 5 =$ ___	g. $1 \times 6 =$ ___	g. $32 / 4 =$ ___
h. $6 \cdot 10 =$ ___	h. $14 \div 2 =$ ___	h. $4 \cdot 3 =$ ___	h. $8 \div 1 =$ ___
i. $9 * 3 =$ ___	i. $27 / 9 =$ ___	i. $7 * 4 =$ ___	i. $24 / 4 =$ ___
j. $2 \times 9 =$ ___	j. $45 / 5 =$ ___	j. $3 \times 7 =$ ___	j. $18 / 3 =$ ___
k. $5 \cdot 8 =$ ___	k. $10 \div 10 =$ ___	k. $0 \cdot 1 =$ ___	k. $10 \div 1 =$ ___
l. $10 * 7 =$ ___	l. $25 / 5 =$ ___	l. $10 * 1 =$ ___	l. $40 / 4 =$ ___
m. $5 \times 5 =$ ___	m. $54 \div 9 =$ ___	m. $4 \times 4 =$ ___	m. $12 \div 3 =$ ___
n. $1 \cdot 5 =$ ___	n. $6 / 2 =$ ___	n. $9 \cdot 3 =$ ___	n. $6 / 3 =$ ___
o. $9 * 6 =$ ___	o. $72 \div 9 =$ ___	o. $8 * 0 =$ ___	o. $4 \div 4 =$ ___
p. $10 \times 10 =$ ___	p. $40 / 5 =$ ___	p. $5 \times 4 =$ ___	p. $7 / 1 =$ ___
q. $4 \cdot 2 =$ ___	q. $80 \div 10 =$ ___	q. $1 \cdot 6 =$ ___	q. $28 \div 4 =$ ___
r. $10 * 8 =$ ___	r. $18 \div 2 =$ ___	r. $3 * 8 =$ ___	r. $24 \div 3 =$ ___
s. $3 \times 9 =$ ___	s. $36 / 9 =$ ___	s. $4 \times 9 =$ ___	s. $20 / 4 =$ ___
t. $9 \cdot 9 =$ ___	t. $30 \div 5 =$ ___	t. $0 \cdot 4 =$ ___	t. $27 \div 3 =$ ___

▶Answers to Dashes 1–4

Use this sheet to check your answers to the Dashes on page 275.

Dash 1 2s, 5s, 9s, 10s Multiplications	Dash 2 2s, 5s, 9s, 10s Divisions	Dash 3 3s, 4s, 0s, 1s Multiplications	Dash 4 3s, 4s, 1s Divisions
a. $4 \times 5 = 20$	a. $8 / 2 = 4$	a. $3 \times 0 = 0$	a. $12 / 4 = 3$
b. $10 \cdot 3 = 30$	b. $50 \div 10 = 5$	b. $4 \cdot 6 = 24$	b. $5 \div 1 = 5$
c. $8 * 9 = 72$	c. $15 / 5 = 3$	c. $9 * 1 = 9$	c. $21 / 3 = 7$
d. $6 \times 2 = 12$	d. $63 \div 9 = 7$	d. $3 \times 3 = 9$	d. $1 \div 1 = 1$
e. $5 \cdot 7 = 35$	e. $90 / 10 = 9$	e. $8 \cdot 4 = 32$	e. $16 / 4 = 4$
f. $10 * 5 = 50$	f. $90 \div 9 = 10$	f. $0 * 5 = 0$	f. $9 \div 3 = 3$
g. $8 \times 2 = 16$	g. $35 / 5 = 7$	g. $1 \times 6 = 6$	g. $32 / 4 = 8$
h. $6 \cdot 10 = 60$	h. $14 \div 2 = 7$	h. $4 \cdot 3 = 12$	h. $8 \div 1 = 8$
i. $9 * 3 = 27$	i. $27 / 9 = 3$	i. $7 * 4 = 28$	i. $24 / 4 = 6$
j. $2 \times 9 = 18$	j. $45 / 5 = 9$	j. $3 \times 7 = 21$	j. $18 / 3 = 6$
k. $5 \cdot 8 = 40$	k. $10 \div 10 = 1$	k. $0 \cdot 1 = 0$	k. $10 \div 1 = 10$
l. $10 * 7 = 70$	l. $25 / 5 = 5$	l. $10 * 1 = 10$	l. $40 / 4 = 10$
m. $5 \times 5 = 25$	m. $54 \div 9 = 6$	m. $4 \times 4 = 16$	m. $12 \div 3 = 4$
n. $1 \cdot 5 = 5$	n. $6 / 2 = 3$	n. $9 \cdot 3 = 27$	n. $6 / 3 = 2$
o. $9 * 6 = 54$	o. $72 \div 9 = 8$	o. $8 * 0 = 0$	o. $4 \div 4 = 1$
p. $10 \times 10 = 100$	p. $40 / 5 = 8$	p. $5 \times 4 = 20$	p. $7 / 1 = 7$
q. $4 \cdot 2 = 8$	q. $80 \div 10 = 8$	q. $1 \cdot 6 = 6$	q. $28 \div 4 = 7$
r. $10 * 8 = 80$	r. $18 \div 2 = 9$	r. $3 * 8 = 24$	r. $24 \div 3 = 8$
s. $3 \times 9 = 27$	s. $36 / 9 = 4$	s. $4 \times 9 = 36$	s. $20 / 4 = 5$
t. $9 \cdot 9 = 81$	t. $30 \div 5 = 6$	t. $0 \cdot 4 = 0$	t. $27 \div 3 = 9$

Answers to Dashes 1–4

Class Activity

Name _____

Date _____

▶ **Solve Word Problems with 2s, 3s, 4s, 5s, 6s, 7s, and 9s**

Solve each problem.

1. Toni counted 36 legs in the lion house at the zoo. How many lions were there?

   _____

2. One wall of an art gallery has a row of 5 paintings and a row of 9 paintings. How many paintings are on the wall?

   _____

3. Josh's muffin pan is an array with 4 rows and 6 columns. How many muffins can Josh make in the pan?

   _____

4. To get ready for the school spelling bee, Tanya studied 3 hours each night for an entire week. How many hours did she study?

   _____

5. The 14 trumpet players in the marching band lined up in 2 equal rows. How many trumpet players were in each row?

   _____

6. The Sunnyside Riding Stable has 9 horses. The owners are going to buy new horseshoes for all the horses. How many horseshoes are needed?

   _____

Name _____   **Date** _____

Going Further

► Use Patterns to Divide 2- and 3-Digit Numbers

Find each quotient.

1. $8 \div 2 = 8$ ones $\div 2 = 4$ ones or _____

    $80 \div 2 = 8$ tens $\div 2 = 4$ tens or _____

    $800 \div 2 = 8$ hundreds $\div 2 = 4$ hundreds or _____

2. $9 \div 3 = 9$ ones $\div 3 =$ _____ ones or _____

    $90 \div 3 = 9$ tens $\div 3 =$ _____ tens or _____

    $900 \div 3 = 9$ hundreds $\div 3 =$ _____ hundreds or _____

3. $8 \div 4 =$ _____   4. $6 \div 2 =$ _____   5. $6 \div 3 =$ _____

    $80 \div 4 =$ _____ $60 \div 2 =$ _____ $60 \div 3 =$ _____

    $800 \div 4 =$ _____ $600 \div 2 =$ _____ $600 \div 3 =$ _____

6. $4 \div 2 =$ _____   7. $9 \div 3 =$ _____   8. $25 \div 5 =$ _____

    $40 \div 2 =$ _____ $90 \div 3 =$ _____ $250 \div 5 =$ _____

    $400 \div 2 =$ _____ $900 \div 3 =$ _____ $2{,}500 \div 5 =$ _____

9. $36 \div 4 =$ _____   10. $72 \div 9 =$ _____   11. $54 \div 9 =$ _____

    $360 \div 4 =$ _____ $720 \div 9 =$ _____ $540 \div 9 =$ _____

    $3{,}600 \div 4 =$ _____ $7{,}200 \div 9 =$ _____ $5{,}400 \div 9 =$ _____

Practice with 0s, 1s, 2s, 3s, 4s, 5s, 9s, and 10s

► **Math and Science**

Apatosaurus   Triceratops   Stegosaurus

Take a survey. Find out which dinosaur is the favorite.

1. What question will you ask?

_____

2. How many people will you ask?

_____

3. Take the survey. Record your results in the tally chart below.

	Tally	Total
Apatosaurus		
Triceratops		
Stegosaurus		

4. Which dinosaur is the favorite? How do you know?

_____

_____

5. What is the difference between the number of votes for the most popular dinosaur and the number of votes for the least popular dinosaur?

_____

► **Take a Survey**

6. What question would you like to ask in a survey?

_____

_____

_____

7. What answer choices will you have in your survey?

_____

_____

_____

8. How many people will you survey?

_____

9. Take the survey. Record your results in the tally chart below.

	Tally	Total

10. Show the results of the survey in a bar graph.
    Use grid paper to make the graph.

11. Make 3 statements about the results of your survey.

_____

_____

_____

Use Mathematical Processes

Multiply or divide.

1. $8 \times 2 =$ ☐

2. $5 \cdot 7 =$ ☐

3. $10 \div 1 =$ ☐

4. $81 \div 9 =$ ☐

5. $4 \times 0 =$ ☐

6. $63 / 9 =$ ☐

7. $6 \cdot 4 =$ ☐

8. $45 / 5 =$ ☐

9. $9 \times 3 =$ ☐

10. $3)\overline{24}$

11. $28 \div 4 =$ ☐

12. $10 * 8 =$ ☐

Write a multiplication equation to find the total number.

13. _____

Without counting the oranges, compare the arrays. Write >, <, or = in the ◯. Then write an equation for each array to show your comparison is correct.

14.

   ◯

_____   _____

Write a multiplication equation to represent the area of the rectangle.

15.   _____

Complete.

16. $9 + 9 + 9 + 9 + 9 + 9 + 9 + 9 =$ _____ $\times\ 9 =$ _____

Write a related division equation.

17. $8 \times 5 = 40$ _____

Write a related multiplication equation.

18. $18 \div 2 = 9$ _____

Write an equation to solve each problem. Then write the answer.

19. Olivia's CD rack has 4 shelves. It holds 8 CDs on a shelf. How many CDs will fit in the rack altogether?

_____

20. **Extended Response** Paco set up 7 tables to seat 28 children at his birthday party. The same number of children will sit at each table. How many children will sit at each table? Explain how you found your answer. Make a math drawing to help explain.

_____

_____

_____

_____

Glossary

A

acute angle An angle whose measure is less than 90°.

acute triangle A triangle in which the measure of each angle is less than 90°.

addend A number to be added.

Example: $8 + 4 = 12$

addend   addend

addition A mathematical operation that combines two or more numbers.

Example: $23 + 52 = 75$

addend   addend   sum

adjacent (sides) Two sides that meet at a point.

Example: Sides *a* and *b* are adjacent.

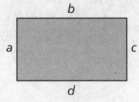

A.M. The time period between midnight and noon.

angle A figure formed by two rays or two line segments that meet at an endpoint.

area The number of square units in a region

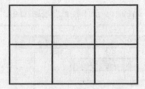

The area of the rectangle is 6 square units.

array An arrangement of objects, pictures, or numbers in columns and rows.

Associative Property of Addition (Grouping Property of Addition) The property which states that changing the way in which addends are grouped does not change the sum.

Example: $(2 + 3) + 1 = 2 + (3 + 1)$

$$5 + 1 = 2 + 4$$

$$6 = 6$$

Associative Property of Multiplication (Grouping Property of Multiplication) The property which states that changing the way in which factors are grouped does not change the product.

Example: $(2 \times 3) \times 4 = 2 \times (3 \times 4)$

$$6 \times 4 = 2 \times 12$$

$$24 = 24$$

Glossary (Continued)

axis (plural: **axes**) A reference line for a graph. A bar graph has 2 axes; one is horizontal and the other is vertical.

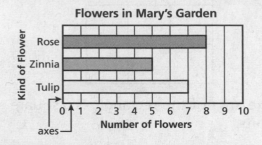

Flowers in Mary's Garden

B

bar graph A graph that uses bars to show data. The bars may be horizontal or vertical.

Canned Goods at Turner's Market

base (of a geometric figure) The bottom side of a 2-D figure or the bottom face of a 3-D figure.

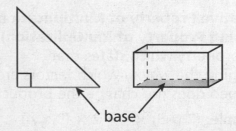

base

C

calculator A tool used to perform mathematical operations.

capacity The amount a container can hold.

cell A rectangle in a table where a column and row meet.

Coin Toss

	Heads	Tails
Sam	11	6
Zoe	9	10

} cell

centimeter (cm) A metric unit used to measure length.

100 cm = 1 m

circle A plane figure that forms a closed path so that all points on the path are the same distance from a point called the center.

circle graph A graph that represents data as parts of a whole.

Jacket Colors in Ms. Timmer's Class

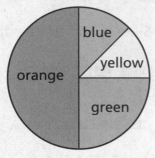

circumference The distance around a circle, about $3\frac{1}{7}$ times the diameter.

column A vertical group of cells in a table.

Coin Toss

	Heads	Tails
Sam	11	6
Zoe	9	10

column

Commutative Property of Addition (Order Property of Addition) The property which states that changing the order of addends does not change the sum.

Example: $3 + 7 = 7 + 3$

$10 = 10$

Commutative Property of Multiplication (Order Property of Multiplication) The property which states that changing the order of factors does not change the product.

Example: $5 \times 4 = 4 \times 5$

$20 = 20$

comparison bars Bars that represent the larger amount, smaller amount, and difference in a comparison problem.

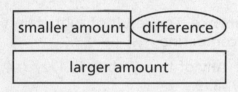

In Volume 2, we use comparison bars for multiplication.

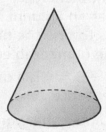

cone A solid figure that has a circular base and comes to a point called the vertex.

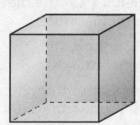

congruent figures Figures that have the same size and shape.

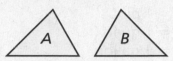

Triangles A and B are congruent.

coordinates The numbers in an ordered pair that locate a point on a coordinate grid. The first number is the distance across and the second number is the distance up.

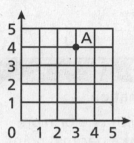

The coordinates 3 and 4 in the ordered pair (3, 4) locate Point A on the coordinate grid.

coordinate grid A grid formed by two perpendicular number lines in which every point is assigned an ordered pair of numbers.

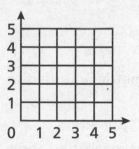

cube A solid figure that has six square faces of equal size.

Glossary (Continued)

cup (c) A customary unit of measurement used to measure capacity.

2 cups = 1 pint
4 cups = 1 quart
16 cups = 1 gallon

cylinder A solid figure with two congruent circular or elliptical faces and one curved surface.

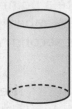

D

data Pieces of information.

decimal A number with one or more digits to the right of a decimal point.
Examples: 1.23 and 0.3

decimal point The dot that separates the whole number from the decimal part.

1.23

↑

decimal point

decimeter (dm) A metric unit used to measure length

1 decimeter = 10 centimeters

degree (°) A unit for measuring angles or temperature.

degrees Celsius (°C) The metric unit for measuring temperature.

degrees Fahrenheit (°F) The customary unit of temperature.

denominator The bottom number in a fraction that shows the total number of equal parts in the whole.
Example: $\frac{1}{3}$ ←——— denominator

diagonal A line segment that connects two corners of a figure and is not a side of the figure.

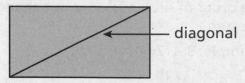

diagonal

diameter A line segment that connects two points on a circle and also passes through the center of the circle. The term is also used to describe the length of such a line segment.

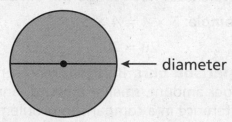

diameter

difference The result of subtraction or of comparing.

digit Any of the symbols 0, 1, 2, 3, 4, 5, 6, 7, 8, 9.

dividend The number that is divided in division.
Examples:

$$12 \div 3 = 4 \qquad 3\overline{)12}^{\,4}$$

↑ ↑

dividend   dividend

division The mathematical operation that separates an amount into smaller equal groups to find the number of groups or the number in each group.
Example: 12 ÷ 3 = 4 is a division number sentence.

divisor The number that you divide by in division.

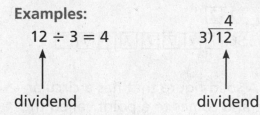

Example: 12 ÷ 3 = 4 $3\overline{)12}^{\,4}$

↑ ↑

divisor   divisor

E

edge The line segment where two faces of a solid figure meet.

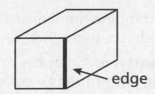

elapsed time The time that passes between the beginning and the end of an activity.

endpoint The point at either end of a line segment or the beginning point of a ray.

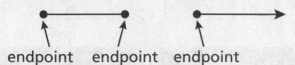

endpoint   endpoint   endpoint

equation A mathematical sentence with an equals sign.

Examples: $11 + 22 = 33$
$75 - 25 = 50$

equilateral triangle A triangle whose sides are all the same length.

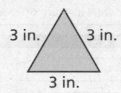

3 in.   3 in.
3 in.

equivalent Equal, or naming the same amount.

equivalent fractions Fractions that name the same amount.

Example: $\frac{1}{2}$ and $\frac{2}{4}$

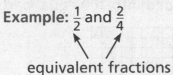

equivalent fractions

estimate About how many or about how much.

even number A whole number that is a multiple of 2. The ones digit in an even number is 0, 2, 4, 6, or 8.

event In probability, a possible outcome.

expanded form A number written to show the value of each of its digits.

Examples:
$347 = 300 + 40 + 7$
$347 = 3$ hundreds $+ 4$ tens $+ 7$ ones

expression A combination of numbers, variables, and/or operation signs. An expression does not have an equals sign.

Examples: $4 + 7$ $a - 3$

F

face A flat surface of a solid figure.

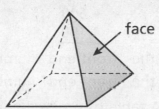

face

factors Numbers that are multiplied to give a product.

Example: $4 \times 5 = 20$

factor   factor   product

flip To reflect a figure over a line. The size and shape of the figure remain the same.

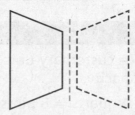

foot (ft) A customary unit used to measure length.

1 foot = 12 inches

Glossary (Continued)

formula An equation with variables that describes a rule.

The formula for the area of a rectangle is:

$A = l \times w$

where A is the area, l is the length, and w is the width.

fraction A number that names part of a whole or part of a set.

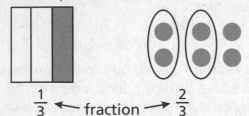

$\frac{1}{3}$ ← fraction → $\frac{2}{3}$

front-end estimation A method of estimating that keeps the largest place value in a number and drops the rest.

Example: 527 → 500
         + 673 → + 600
         _____   1,100

The 5 in 527 is the "front end" number

The 6 in 673 is the "front end" number

function table A table of ordered pairs that shows a function.

For every input number, there is only one possible output number.

Rule: add 2	
Input	Output
1	3
2	4
3	5
4	6

G
---

gallon (gal) A customary unit used to measure capacity.

1 gallon = 4 quarts = 8 pints = 16 cups

gram (g) A metric unit of mass, about 1 paper clip.

1,000 grams = 1 kilogram

greater than (>) A symbol used to compare two numbers.

Example: 6 > 5
         6 is greater than 5.

group To combine numbers to form new tens, hundreds, thousands, and so on.

growing pattern A number or geometric pattern that increases.

Examples: 2, 4, 6, 8, 10...
          1, 2, 5, 10, 17...

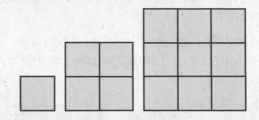

H
---

height A measurement of vertical length, or how tall something is.

horizontal Extending in two directions, left and right.

horizontal bar graph A bar graph with horizontal bars.

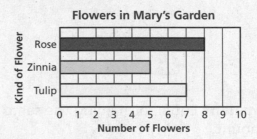

hundredth One of the equal parts when a whole is divided into 100 equal parts.

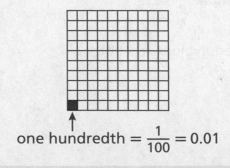

one hundredth $= \frac{1}{100} = 0.01$

I

improper fraction A fraction in which the numerator is equal to or is greater than the denominator. Improper fractions are equal to or greater than 1. $\frac{5}{5}$ and $\frac{8}{3}$ are improper fractions.

inch (in.) A customary unit used to measure length.

12 inches = 1 foot

isosceles triangle A triangle that has at least two sides of the same length.

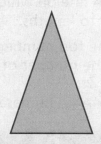

K

key A part of a map, graph, or chart that explains what symbols mean.

kilogram (kg) A metric unit of mass.

1 kilogram = 1,000 grams

kilometer (km) A metric unit of length.

1 kilometer = 1,000 meters

L

less than (<) A symbol used to compare numbers.

Example: 5 < 6
　　　　　5 *is less than* 6.

line A straight path that goes on forever in opposite directions.

line graph A graph that uses a straight line or a broken line to show changes in data.

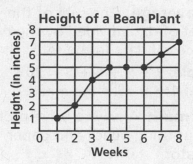
Height of a Bean Plant

line of symmetry A line on which a figure can be folded so that the two halves match exactly.

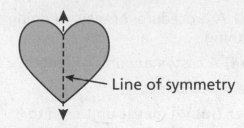
Line of symmetry

line plot A way to show data using a number line.

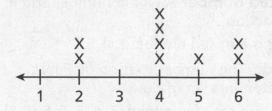

line segment A part of a line. A line segment has two endpoints.

liter (L) A metric unit used to measure capacity.

1 liter = 1,000 milliliters

Glossary (Continued)

M

mass The amount of matter in an object.

mean (average) The sum of the values in a set of data divided by the number of pieces of data in the set.

Example: $3 + 5 + 4 + 8 = 20$
$20 \div 4 = 5$ 5 is the mean

mental math A way to solve problems without using pencil and paper, or a calculator.

meter (m) A metric unit used to measure length.

1 meter = 100 centimeters

method A procedure, or way, of doing something.

mile (mi) A customary unit of length.

1 mile = 5,280 feet

milliliter (mL) A metric unit used to measure capacity.

1,000 milliliters = 1 liter

mixed number A whole number and a fraction.

$1\frac{3}{4}$ is a mixed number.

mode The number that occurs most often in a set of data.

In this set of numbers {3, 4, 5, 5, 5, 7, 8}, 5 is the mode.

multiple A number that is the product of the given number and another number.

multiplication A mathematical operation that combines equal groups.

Example: $4 \times 3 = 12$

factor factor product

$3 + 3 + 3 + 3 = 12$

4 times

N

net A flat pattern that can be folded to make a solid figure.

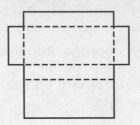

This net can be folded into a rectangular prism.

number line A line on which numbers are assigned to lengths.

numerator The top number in a fraction that shows the number of equal parts counted.

Example: $\frac{1}{3}$ ⟵ numerator

O

obtuse angle An angle that measures more than 90° but less than 180°.

obtuse triangle A triangle with one angle that measures more than 90°.

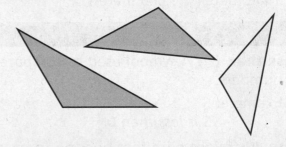

odd number A whole number that is not a multiple of 2. The ones digit in an odd number is 1, 3, 5, 7, or 9.

opposite sides Sides that are across from each other; they do not meet at a point.

Example: Sides *a* and *c* are opposite.

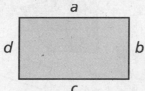

ordered pair A pair of numbers such as (3, 4) in which one number is considered to be first and the other number second. They can name a point on a coordinate grid.

ordinal numbers Numbers used to show order or position.

Example: first, second, fifth

ounce (oz) A customary unit used to measure weight.

16 ounces = 1 pound

P

parallel lines Two lines that are everywhere the same distance apart.

parallelogram A quadrilateral with both pairs of opposite sides parallel.

partner One of two numbers that add to make a total.

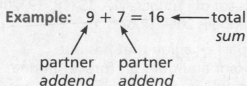
Example: 9 + 7 = 16 ←——total
sum
partner partner
addend *addend*

perimeter The distance around the outside of a figure.

perpendicular Two lines or line segments that cross or meet to form right angles.

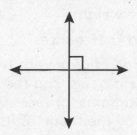

pictograph A graph that uses pictures or symbols to represent data.

pint (pt) A customary unit used to measure capacity.

1 pint = 2 cups

place value The value assigned to the place that a digit occupies in a number.

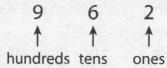
9   6   2
↑   ↑   ↑
hundreds tens ones

place value drawing A drawing that represents a number. Hundreds are represented by boxes, tens by vertical lines, and ones by small circles.

962

plane figure A closed figure that has two dimensions.

Glossary (Continued)

P.M. The time period between noon and midnight.

pound (lb) A customary unit used to measure weight.

1 pound = 16 ounces

prism A solid figure with two parallel congruent bases, and rectangles or parallelograms for faces. A prism is named by the shape of its bases.

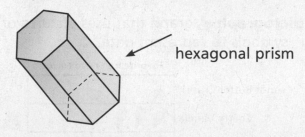

hexagonal prism

probability The chance of an event occurring.

product The answer when you multiply numbers.

Example: 4 × 7 = 28

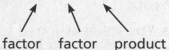

factor   factor   product

proof drawing A drawing used to show that an answer is correct.

```
  249
+ 386
  11
  635
```

pyramid A solid figure with one base and whose other faces are triangles with a common vertex. A pyramid is named by the shape of its base.

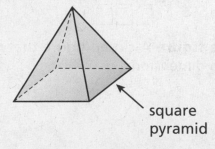

square pyramid

quadrilateral A figure with four sides.

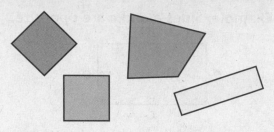

quart (qt) A customary unit used to measure capacity.

1 quart = 4 cups

quotient The answer when you divide numbers.

Examples:

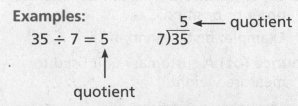

35 ÷ 7 = 5

quotient

radius A line segment that connects the center of a circle to any point on the circle. The term is also used to describe the length of such a line segment.

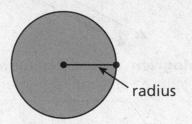

radius

range The difference between the greatest number and the least number in a set of data.

In this set of numbers {12, 15, 18, 19, 20}, the range is 20 − 12 or 8

ray A part of a line that has one endpoint and goes on forever in one direction.

rectangle A parallelogram that has 4 right angles.

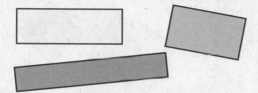

rectangular prism A prism with six rectangular faces.

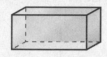

rectangular pyramid A pyramid with a rectangular base and four triangular faces.

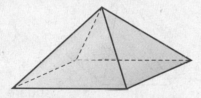

repeating pattern A pattern consisting of a group of numbers, letters, or figures that repeat.
Examples: 1, 2, 1, 2, …
　　　　 A, B, C, A, B, C, …

rhombus A parallelogram with congruent sides.

right angle An angle that measures 90°.

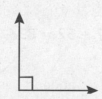

right triangle A triangle with one right angle.

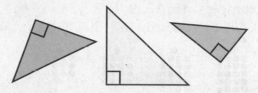

round To find about how many or how much by expressing a number to the nearest ten, hundred, thousand, and so on.

route The path taken to get to a location.

row A horizontal group of cells in a table.

Coin Toss

	Heads	Tails
Sam	11	6
Zoe	9	10

} row

S

scale An arrangement of numbers in order with equal intervals.

scalene triangle A triangle with sides of three different lengths.

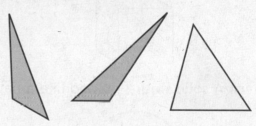

Glossary (Continued)

shrinking pattern A number or geometric pattern that decreases.

Examples: 15, 12, 9, 6, 3,…
25, 20, 16, 13, 11,…

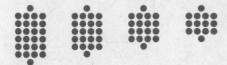

side (of a figure) A line segment that makes up a figure.

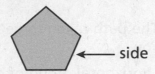

side

simplify To write an equivalent fraction with a smaller numerator and denominator.

slide To move a figure along a line in any direction. The size and shape of the figure remain the same.

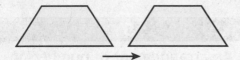

solid figure A figure that has three dimensions.

sphere A solid figure shaped like a ball.

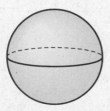

square A rectangle with four sides of the same length.

square number A product of a whole number and itself.

Example: $4 \times 4 = 16$

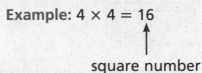

square number

square pyramid A pyramid with a square base and four triangular faces.

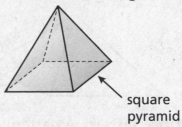

square pyramid

standard form The name of a number written using digits.

Example: 1,829

straight angle An angle that measures 180°.

subtract To find the difference of two numbers.

Example: $18 - 11 = 7$

subtraction A mathematical operation on a sum (total) and an addend, which can be called the difference.

Example: $43 - 40 = 3$

sum The answer when adding two or more addends.

Example: $37 + 52 = 89$

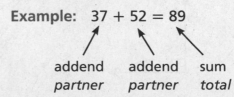

addend   addend   sum
partner   *partner*   *total*

survey A method of collecting information.

symmetry A figure has symmetry if it can be folded along a line so that the two halves match exactly.

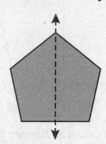

T

table An easy to read arrangement of data, usually in rows and columns.

Coin Toss

	Heads	Tails
Sam	11	6
Zoe	9	10

tally marks Short line segments drawn in groups of 5. Each mark including the slanted marks stands for 1 unit.

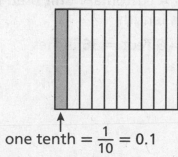

means 13

tenth One of the equal parts when a whole is divided into ten equal parts.

one tenth = $\frac{1}{10}$ = 0.1

thermometer A tool for measuring temperature.

total The answer when adding two or more addends. The sum of two or more numbers.

Example: 672 + 228 = 900

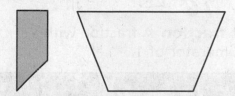

partner *addend* partner *addend* total *sum*

trapezoid A quadrilateral with exactly one pair of parallel sides.

triangular prism A solid figure with two triangular faces and three rectangular faces.

Example:

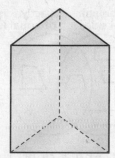

triangular pyramid A pyramid whose base is a triangle.

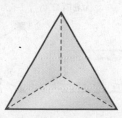

turn To rotate a figure around a point. The size and shape of the figure remains the same.

Glossary (Continued)

U

ungroup To open up 1 in a given place to make 10 of the next smaller place value in order to subtract.

unit fraction A fraction with a numerator of 1.

V

Venn diagram A diagram that uses circles to show the relationship among sets of objects.

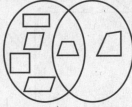

At least one pair of parallel sides   Exactly two sides of equal length

vertex A point where sides, rays, or edges meet.

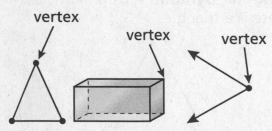

vertex   vertex   vertex

vertical Extending in two directions, up and down.

vertical bar graph A bar graph with vertical bars.

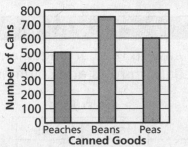

Canned Goods at Turner's Market

W

weight The measure of how heavy something is.

word form A name of a number written using words instead of digits.

Example: Nine hundred eighty-four

Y

yard (yd) A customary unit used to measure length.

1 yard = 3 feet = 36 inches